Common Crisis
North–South:
Cooperation for world
recovery

Common Crisis
North–South:
Cooperation for world
recovery

The Brandt Commission

Willy Brandt

Abdlatif Y. Al-Hamad	(Kuwait)
Rodrigo Botero Montoya	(Colombia)
Antoine Kipsa Dakouré	(Upper Volta)
Eduardo Frei Montalva (1911-1982)	(Chile)
Katharine Graham	(USA)
Edward Heath	(UK)
Amir H. Jamal	(Tanzania)
Lakshmi Kant Jha	(India)
Khatijah Ahmad	(Malaysia)
Adam Malik	(Indonesia)
Haruki Mori	(Japan)
Joe Morris	(Canada)
Olof Palme	(Sweden)
Peter G. Peterson*	(USA)
Edgard Pisani	(France)
Shridath Ramphal	(Guyana)
Layachi Yaker	(Algeria)

Ex officio Members

Jan Pronk	(Netherlands)
Goran Ohlin	(Sweden)
Dragoslav Avramović	(Yugoslavia)

*Mr Peterson did not participate in
the preparation of this Memorandum.

The MIT Press
Cambridge, Massachusetts

The map on the front cover is based upon the Peters Projection rather than the more familiar Mercator Projection.

The Peters Projection introduces several innovative characteristics: an accurate rendition of the proportion of the land surface area; graphical representation of the entire world surface, including the polar regions; the Equator is placed at the centre of the map; the usual grid of 180 Meridians (East and West) and 90 Meridians each (North and South) is replaced by a decimal degree network dividing the earth both East and West and North and South into 100 fields each; angle accuracy in the main North-South, East-West directions.

The surface distortions that do appear are distributed at the Equator and the poles; the more densely settled earth zones, it is claimed, appear in proper proportion to each other. This projection represents an important step away from the prevailing Eurocentric geographical and cultural concept of the world.

The map is printed courtesy of Dr Arno Peters of the University of Bremen.

First MIT Press paperback edition, 1983

First published 1983 by Pan Books Ltd,
Cavaye Place, London SW10 9PG
© The Independent Bureau on International Development Issues 1983

Set, printed, and bound in the United States of America

ISBN 0-262-52085-0
Library of Congress catalog card number: 83-60614

In Memoriam
Eduardo Frei Montalva
1911-1982

Contents

Abbreviations

The following are the main abbreviations used in the text:

CIEC	Conference on International Economic Cooperation
CMEA	Council for Mutual Economic Assistance (also known as Comecon)
EEC	European Economic Community
FAO	Food and Agriculture Organization of the United Nations
GATT	General Agreement on Tariffs and Trade
GSP	Generalized System of Preferences
IBRD	International Bank for Reconstruction and Development (also known as the World Bank)
IDA	International Development Association
ILO	International Labour Office/Organization
IMF	International Monetary Fund
ODA	Official Development Assistance
OECD	Organization for Economic Cooperation and Development
OPEC	Organization of Petroleum Exporting Countries
UNCTAD	United Nations Conference on Trade and Development
UNDP	United Nations Development Programme
UNEP	United Nations Environment Programme
UNESCO	United Nations Educational, Scientific and Cultural Organization
UNIDO	United Nations Industrial Development Organization
WHO	World Health Organization
WIPO	World Intellectual Property Organization

Common Crisis
North–South:
Cooperation for world
recovery

Introduction: Willy Brandt

It is three years now since we published our Report *North–South: A Programme for Survival*. Recent developments, unfortunately, served to confirm some of the worst fears expressed in that Report. The world's prospects have deteriorated rapidly: not only for improved relations between industrialised and developing countries, but for the outlook of the world economy as a whole. The long-run implications of failure to act, referred to in our Report, have been further spelled out in another document, the *Global 2000* report published in the USA in 1980. Deteriorating economic conditions already threaten the political stability of developing countries. Further decline is likely to cause the disintegration of societies and create conditions of anarchy in many parts of the world.

My colleagues and I, as former members of the Independent Commission on International Development Issues, felt it necessary to present an urgent and up-to-date version of our original Emergency Programme. On our evaluation of the world crisis and on our key proposals we are in unanimous agreement. The other parts of the document are also the result of common thinking, though not all members of our group may agree fully with each particular sentence.

To implement these measures, we appeal to governments and international institutions, leaders in business and politics, concerned citizens and non-governmental organisations. The first copy of this Memorandum, like the earlier Report, will be presented to the UN Secretary General.

Most of what we said three years ago is even more to the point now. The international community has made little headway in tackling its most serious problems – which begin in the strained system of international economic relations and result in additional burdens on many developing countries. Prospects for the future are alarming. Increased global uncertainties have reduced expectations of economic growth even more, and the problem of managing the international imbalances of payments is increasing the threat of grave crises in international finance. We have serious doubts as to whether the existing world machinery can cope with these imbalances and the management of world liquidity and debt.

Some steps are presently being considered by the international community, and some of our earlier proposals have been accepted. But a real breakthrough has not been achieved. In particular, the North–South Summit at Cancun, Mexico, in the fall of 1981, which we had proposed in our Report, fell far short of our expectations. It produced no new guidelines nor any clear impetus for future negotiations. It did not even come close to launching the idea of a world economic recovery programme.

When we published our Report we believed nations should urgently start taking concrete steps toward improving constructive North–South cooperation, without which the world economic situation could only deteriorate further, and possibly result in conflict and catastrophe.

We believe such action to be even more urgent now.

It was in a spirit of concern but also of hope that we presented the proposals contained in our Report. We have not given up hope; but today we see far greater dangers than three years ago.

We believe that the world's economic and monetary system must now be reconsidered and restructured under circumstances nearly as serious as those of 1944, when the lingering horrors of 1930s economic disasters inspired the new Bretton Woods institutions – GATT, IMF, and World

Bank. The vision and need for a new economic order were clear then. In the words of Harry Dexter White, the American counterpart of Lord Keynes at Bretton Woods, who criticised his government's attitude:

Where modern diplomacy calls for swift and bold action, we engage in long drawn-out cautious negotiation; where we should talk in terms of billions of dollars, we think in terms of millions; where we should measure success by the generosity of the government that can best afford it, we measure it by the sharpness of the bargain driven; where we should be dealing with all-embracing economic, political and social problems, we discuss minor trade objectives, or small national advantages; . . . we must substitute, before it is too late, imagination for tradition; generosity for shrewdness; understanding for bargaining; toughness for caution; and wisdom for prejudice. We are rich – we should use more of our wealth in the interest of peace.

Our earlier report met with a good reception. It reached a large audience in many parts of the world and is now available in over twenty languages, including Arabic, Chinese, Swahili and Romanian. (Details are given in the Annexe.) As a result of the interest aroused by the Report, members of the Commission, which ceased to exist as a formal body after the Report was adopted, were invited to address interested groups in one country after another. This response, and the widespread public demand expressed through an avalanche of letters and invitations to individual members, kept the group alive and enabled us to engage in continuous thinking both on the problems covered in the Report and on international developments since its publication.

The Report received support from concerned citizens as well as governments in both the developing and developed countries. It had only a limited impact in some countries – notably the United States – but in others the public reaction was most impressive. At our first follow-up meeting in The Hague, for example, the Report was discussed at a public meeting with almost 4,000 participants. In London a mass lobby on Parliament of some 10,000 supporters of the Report's proposals actually led to a change in government attitudes. Our meeting in Berlin led to a new surge of interest in Germany and a pocket book edition of the Report was published. The Report was also debated in the parliaments of many countries, and in the European Parliament. The international trade union movement, church groups and the world organisation of Junior Chambers of Commerce, among others, made the Report a focal point of their work. At the United Nations Special Sessions in 1981, many representatives referred to the Report and called for the implementation of its suggestions.

In the Soviet Union and other East European countries there were only limited signs of positive discussion on the issues raised in our Report (although it has been translated into Romanian and a Polish translation may still be forthcoming). In the People's Republic of China the translation of the Report and its publication in 1981 were arranged with the assistance of the government. In 1980 that country assumed the Chinese seat in the International Monetary Fund and the World Bank. Since that time Hungary joined both institutions, and Poland began its application for membership.

On the governmental level, the Austrian Chancellor Bruno Kreisky and the Mexican President Lopez Portillo, with strong support from the Canadian Prime Minister Pierre Trudeau, organised the Cancun Summit recommended in our Report. Addressing itself to the issues which we had identified in our Emergency Programme, this summit, the largest ever devoted exclusively to North–South issues, seemed to reflect a consensus of world leaders on the necessity for new initiatives in the fields of food and energy – and for launching global negotiations.

But after Cancun there was a setback. Most industrialised countries, facing deteriorating economic conditions at home, adopted self-centred measures – with dramatic and damaging side-effects on North–South economic cooperation.

When we met in Kuwait at the beginning of 1982 we felt it our duty to reassess, reiterate and where necessary revise our earlier recommendations in light of the worsening dilemma. We believed that the kind of uncoordinated policies which industrialised countries were following was not only harming the Third World, but could lead the whole world into a depression comparable only to the crisis of half a century ago. On the other hand, North–South cooperation, with appropriate policies, could stimulate world economic recovery.

Thus we have taken a fresh look at our earlier proposals, adjusted and updated in light of recent developments, and are focusing now on the Emergency Programme. We have tried to spell out these proposals in greater detail, with the hope and expectation that an increased common awareness of the problems may bring about a meeting of minds – without which we will all become victims of regrettable events. We reaffirm our conviction that change is inevitable. Will the world community take deliberate and decisive steps to bring it about, or will change be forced upon us all through circumstances over which the international community will have little control? There is still a chance to decide. But time is short, and every day may count.

What procedural steps could we take to overcome the inertia and forestall these dangers?

Together with my colleagues I believe in doing first things first. We must not, of course, lose sight of the longer-term objectives, and I continue to be a strong supporter of what is envisaged under the proposed 'global negotiations' in the United Nations. ('Global negotiations', within the framework of the United Nations, is the code name of a most ambitious project for discussing the entire range of North–South issues among all the nations, with the support and collaboration of the relevant international agencies. The aim of 'global negotiations' is international consensus. This means that no single problem, energy or debt or food, for example,

5

would be viewed in isolation without considering its direct implications on the full global agenda of interconnected issues.)

But I am also a realist, and I know that such negotiations – if they finally get started – will take some time, several years without doubt. In the meantime a great deal could be done and much action taken on many fronts – as we propose in this Memorandum.

● The emergency measures proposed in this Memorandum should be part of the agenda of forthcoming international meetings. For example, its main elements could be adopted at the next meeting of the United Nations Conference on Trade and Development (UNCTAD VI) in Belgrade, in June 1983.

● Interested countries should take steps as soon as possible to initiate international economic consultations to prepare the emergency measures for immediate implementation – without delay and without waiting for the results of global negotiations which will take several years. These should include measures in the fields of finance and trade, the creation of the requisite institutional improvements for dealing with investments in the energy sector, the stabilisation of commodity markets, and a substantial increase in the flow of resources to developing countries. (These would all be steps towards, and not alternatives to, the creation of what is called in the United Nations a 'new international economic order', a system of international relations acceptable to the great majority of countries and not biased against weaker nations.) All these measures we see as valuable to the South, but also contributing to recovery and employment in the North.

● A special overviewing group could be set up, perhaps on the initiative of the UN Secretary General, to assist in clearing the procedural steps for setting in motion the long overdue 'global negotiations' and – in parallel – to assist the process of implementing emergency measures to meet the current crisis.

● And it may be worthwhile to consider yet another North–South Summit meeting, despite the unsatisfactory outcome of the first one. Greater attention could be paid to our initial suggestion of limiting it to 'some twenty-five leaders . . . to enable initiatives and concessions to be thrashed out with candour and boldness'. (At Cancun, each participating country was represented around the conference table by the head of state or government plus three officials, and almost the entire first day of the two-day meeting was spent reading prepared statements.)

It is relevant to draw attention to the Report of the Independent Commission on Disarmament and Security Issues under the chairmanship of Olof Palme, who is also a member of our Commission. Their report, *Common Security*, was published in early 1982. It analyses, among other important issues, the economic impact of military expenditures. *Common Security* points out how the weapons burden is straining even the wealthiest economies and how increasingly it threatens the stability of states and societies irrespective of ideology or system of government.

In 1982, at a time when other tensions were perhaps even more dangerous than the East–West conflict, $650 billion were spent world-wide on military purposes, adding to an arsenal already capable of destroying humankind many times over. This escalation has an indisputable link with the problems with which our Commission has been dealing. We need substantial investment in development in order to make the transition to a reasonably stable world of ten or fifteen billion people by the next century. Mobilising the enormous amount of capital required would be likely to involve at least a partial shift of budgetary funds from military spending to development spending. It is high time to take note of this link at the negotiations on arms limitation.

There are some indications today that the intolerable economic burdens of the arms race, as well as the military dangers, have caused both superpowers to be more seriously concerned with the attainment of an effective arms control policy leading to disarmament.

There is no doubt in my mind: only an end to the arms race, which in developing countries also has reached a terrifying pace, will give us the chance of overcoming our common crisis – the grim political and economic confusion engulfing our societies everywhere.

This Memorandum deals only with some of the urgent issues. We believe that the present technological revolution has huge implications in bridging different systems, while the threat to the environment, and its destruction, have become even more serious. We have learned how difficult it is to contain the excessive growth of world population and how shortsighted it is to neglect the social implications of applying necessary economic measures, or to forget that development for many people also means fulfilling their own cultural aspirations.

What limits our response to the challenge of the present crisis? As we said in our earlier Report: it is not primarily the lack of technical solutions, which are already largely familiar, but the lack of a clear and broadly reflected awareness of the current realities and dangers, and an absence of the political will necessary to meet the real problems. Only a new spirit of solidarity, based on a respect for the individual, the national heritage and the common good, can make possible the achievement of the solutions so desperately needed.

We must all make adjustment and sacrifice: we must correct injustice and inequality both internationally and within nations. The burdens will doubtless be greater for those with more power and resources to bear them; but no nation or group of nations will in the end be able to save itself either by dominion over others or by isolation from them. Real progress can be made nationally only if it is assured globally. This is the inevitable reality of the growing interdependence of today's world.

A global approach is essential. It cannot be limited to economic problems. But without solving the economic we can hardly overcome the other difficulties. The basis of any world order – or any national or regional order – must be respect for individual people and their essential rights, as defined in the Universal Declaration of Human Rights. Otherwise, there would be no true economic and social development and, above all, no justice, freedom or peace.

Our situation is unique. Never before was the survival of mankind itself at stake; and never before was mankind capable of destroying itself, not only as the possible outcome of a world-wide arms race, but as a result of uncontrolled exploitation and destruction of global resources as well. We may be arming ourselves to death without actually going to war – by strangling our economies and refusing to invest in the future. Everybody knows – or should know – where the world economic crisis of the 1930s ended. Everybody should know what immense dangers the present international crisis holds, and that only a new relationship between industrialised countries and developing countries can help overcome this crisis. There is a clear common interest. This, of course, does not reduce the moral obligation of the rich to the poor, in particular towards those whose situations have become more desperate in the last few years.

We still have a chance. But we must lift our sights to the far horizons. We need courage and imagination; we must cooperate and overcome narrow-mindedness; and we must take bold action now. Today, responsible women and men, and the younger generation above all, realise in their daily lives that their own condition is no longer isolated: their jobs, their food, their energy – even the solvency of their local bank – depend upon and influence the development of people, communities, and countries at the other end of the world.

May they all try to understand and to conduct their affairs in the light of this new challenge. For without wide recognition and support from every sphere – global, regional, and especially at local levels – our proposals will have little impact, countries will pursue their own interests, and the world will hasten its march to oblivion. We too often forget that even today the depth of human suffering is immense. Every two seconds of this year a child will die of hunger or disease. And no statistic can express what it is to see even one child die . . . 'to see the uncomprehending panic in eyes which are still the clear and lucid eyes of a child'.

Together with my colleagues I hold the hope that the thoughts we have set forth may light a pathway to a more just and prosperous world for generations to come – free from dependence and oppression, from hunger and distress. A new century nears, and with it the prospects of a new civilisation. Could we not begin to lay the basis for that new community with reasonable relations among all people and nations, and to build a world in which sharing, justice, freedom, and peace might prevail?

Ottawa, December 1982

1 The Setting: Three Years Later

Three years have passed since the publication of the Brandt Commission's Report: *North–South: A Programme for Survival* – years which have brought increasing economic hardship to the industrial countries, and little short of disaster to much of the developing world.

The Commission foresaw the world community in the 1980s facing much greater dangers than at any time since the Second World War. The prospects are now even darker. The international recession, which could deepen into depression in 1983; massive unemployment in the North and the threat of economic collapse in parts of the South; the acute dangers to the world's financial system and growing disorder in international trade; the deterioration of East–West relations and renewed arms build-ups; political and economic crises within Eastern Europe and at many other points in the globe; wars and civil strife in many Third World countries – all these add up to a highly unstable and uncertain future.

At the same time the Commission offered hope. It expressed the belief that national problems could be solved, but only with a degree of collaboration and wider vision which is still lacking in international affairs. It also argued that nations should perceive their mutual interest in taking joint action. That perception has for the most part been lacking – or if it was there, it was overwhelmed by other events and other interests. But today it is self-evident.

The Commission's Report has been influential in securing a wider public hearing for North–South issues and raising the political level at which they are discussed. The Cancum Summit which brought world leaders together to consider them was the first of its kind and was a direct result of the Report. The leaders present felt that their exchanges had been valuable, but while the Summit helped to keep alive the process of Global Negotiations within the United Nations, it did not make any immediate contribution to resolving the problems of developing countries; nor did it set up any continuing procedure to accelerate negotiations.

The Summit took place in October 1981. Now, more than a year later, there is still little sign of action. The North–South dialogue remains much where it was when the Commission reported. Some modest steps forward have been taken. And some backwards. Meanwhile the world economy continues its dangerous downward slide, and the desperate situation of many developing countries finds no new hope of relief.

Crisis induces an impulse to contract. But this is already a crisis of contraction: contraction of production, of employment, of trade, of credit, of aid, of economic growth. And it is a common crisis; it afflicts rich and poor; market, mixed and centrally planned economies; industrial and agricultural communities. If each country retreats inwards out of an impulse of self-preservation we shall end up hurting each other and worsening both our collective and individual condition. This common crisis demands a collective response – one that must be made with imagination, intelligence and courage, and made quickly. There is not much more time to take the policy measures necessary to avert a major world depression.

This was the background against which Commission members came together and decided to publish a second document, with the aim of raising public consciousness of the gravity of the common crisis and making proposals to redress it.

In doing so we in no way imply any diminution of our commitment to the proposals contained in our Report. They must in our view remain the goals towards which

12

international cooperation is directed. We attach continuing importance to what we described as a programme of priorities – tasks for the 1980s and 1990s. The Emergency Programme in our Report was not put forward as a substitute for the longer-term programme of priority reforms; nor are the emergency measures in this Memorandum. Indeed, we have been careful to ensure their consistency with those necessary longer-term measures of reform.

Main Proposals

Our proposals are directed to averting world economic collapse and the subsequent chaos and human suffering and to creating conditions leading to world economic recovery. We seek to restore confidence in the banking system; to avoid the strangulation of world trade through increased protectionism and to move it back into growth; to make developing countries more self-sufficient in food and energy production; and to improve the negotiating process between North and South. We insist that longer-term measures of reform will be essential to the international financial and trading system, without which recovery and growth could not be sustained. But our measures constitute the minimum emergency action which we believe nations must now take together.

Finance
Finance is central to most of these measures. We call on governments and world leaders to take immediate action to:

● Increase the resources of the IMF by:
  (i) a major new allocation of Special Drawing Rights, distributed on a basis which takes into account the particular needs of developing countries in deficit. Such an increase in SDRs, which are essentially lines of credit honoured by IMF member countries,[1] would take into account the deepening recession, reduced inflation, falling reserves,

13

declining international liquidity, and the urgent need for recovery – all conditions which, according to the IMF Articles of Agreement, justify new SDR allocations;

(ii) taking action to secure at least a doubling of IMF quotas;

(iii) increased borrowing from central banks, particularly those of surplus countries;

(iv) borrowing from capital markets.

● Make more funds available from the IMF's low conditionality tranches, and from the Compensatory Financing Facility, thereby encouraging countries to come to the Fund earlier.

● Hold an emergency meeting of the Governors of the IMF to consider the above proposals in the light of the first 1983 meeting of the Interim Committee.

● Enable the Bank for International Settlements and the central banks of major countries to give greater assistance to developing countries by extending bridging finance between the time when a country approaches the IMF and when it receives its first disbursement.

● Increase the World Bank group's overall resources for both programme lending and project lending; and facilitate an enlargement of its programme lending, including lending for structural adjustment, by raising its present limit on such lending from 10 per cent to at least 30 per cent of total lending.

● Make a strong commitment to a real increase in funds for the Seventh IDA replenishment.

● Raise aid levels for low-income countries; and implement fully the agreement at the UN Conference on Least Developed Countries, namely, to provide 0.15 per cent of GNP or a doubling of aid to these countries by 1985. This and the Seventh IDA replenishment would be part of an effort to meet the 0.7-per-cent aid target in the space of five years.

● Fulfil earlier undertakings regarding official debt by ensuring that all such debts to all least developed countries are waived.

- Strengthen informal coordination among the IMF, the World Bank, other official lenders and the commercial banks in negotiations on debt rescheduling or to overcome severe financial difficulties, to ensure adequate provision of resources through the support of all lenders.

Trade

World trade is stagnating, and there is growing disregard for the rules of the trading system. This Memorandum discusses the international agenda on trade for the immediate future. But as matters of priority we call for:

- Reinforcement of the undertaking given by industrialised countries at the GATT Ministerial Meeting to resist protectionist pressures.
- Early completion of negotiations for an improved safeguards code.
- Ratification of the Common Fund; negotiation of new International Commodity Agreements; and increased compensation for periodic losses of developing countries' commodity export earnings.

Food

There is grave concern at the growing food deficits in many developing countries and the rapid growth in the cost of food imports. We therefore propose measures to increase and improve resource flows to agriculture, especially through support for national food strategies; to strengthen the system of international food security; to combat ecological deterioration; to support a major expansion of agricultural research, especially for African countries; and to increase food aid while monitoring it to avoid its possible disincentive effect on food production.

Energy

To help developing countries produce more of their own energy, and to reduce instability in world energy markets, we propose: a new energy agency to increase energy self-reliance in developing countries; institutional and financial support for energy research and the dissemination of its results; and a dialogue between major oil-producing and oil-consuming countries to consider arrangements beneficial to all parties, including safeguarding supplies to the poorest countries.

The negotiating process
Lastly we propose measures to improve the process of negotiation between North and South, which has itself become an obstacle to progress on the crucial issues confronting the world economy. We call for changes in attitudes and procedures on the part of both North and South, including more readiness to negotiate in small groups and on single issues within the framework of universal fora. Given such changes, and more determined leadership by the 'like-minded' countries, we would expect that a new Global Round of Negotiations in the United Nations could bear fruit; and we call for it to proceed. We also propose a second North–South Summit with adequate advance preparation to give new impetus to international economic negotiations. But in the immediate future we call for urgent world economic consultations on the adoption and implementation of emergency measures for recovery and development, bearing in mind the opportunities offered by the Sixth Session of UNCTAD which is to take place in Yugoslavia in June 1983.

The World Economy

The world economy faces its fourth consecutive year of stagnation. It could well contract further. The great majority of the world's countries, North and South, are deliberately restraining economic activity, and are trying to limit imports and expand exports. But they are mainly communicating to each other the ill effects of their policies.

The North
The industrial countries have aimed to control their

inflation and bring it down to the point where inflationary expectations are dampened or if possible extinguished. But many countries have attacked the problem with excessive concentration on monetary control, often accompanied by perverse fiscal policies. And the disregard both of objectives other than the control of inflation and of the international consequences of policy has now produced heavy unemployment and all the symptoms of economic decay. With so little effort at international coordination, the results have been more painful than was necessary.

High interest rates in the United States forced other countries to maintain higher rates than they would have wished, in order to avoid currency outflows and depreciating exchange rates. Mismatch of policies internationally has also caused wide swings in the value of major countries' currencies in recent years, which added to uncertainty and further worsened the climate for investment and trade. A number of countries – particularly those such as Japan and the Federal Republic of Germany whose trade surpluses should have given them more room for manoeuvre – have had to accept unnecessarily restrictive policies, and slower growth. The OECD now forecasts growth at 1.5 per cent for member countries' economies in 1983; but in 1981 they forecast similar growth for 1982, which proved to be a year of decline. Unemployment is forecast to rise to 35 million by 1984.[2] Certainly without changes in policies and greater consultation and cooperation among countries it is hard to see where more rapid growth will come from.

The South
Industrial economies transmit their troubles to developing countries by a number of routes. Uncoordinated policies in the North to eliminate payments deficits due to oil price increases or to reduce inflation have increased the adjustment burden on oil-importing developing countries. For the poorer countries this burden has been particularly severe because the recession has dramatically reduced their commodity export earnings, and they cannot borrow to

finance deficits. But for other countries too debt service payments have risen steeply as a result of high interest rates, and increased borrowing is becoming difficult to sustain. Even the better-off developing countries are now reducing imports, which further aggravates the recession.

In fact the developing countries today are, with few exceptions, in a desperate plight. With the prices of commodities – the main exports of many countries – at their lowest level for over thirty years, recession and protectionism affecting their exports of manufactures, a slowing up in the flow of commercial capital and aid, their balance of payments problems have reached intolerable proportions. Cutting back on growth is the order of the day – for those countries which have been growing. For numerous countries – especially in Sub-Saharan Africa, where there has been no growth in recent years – lack of capacity to import translates directly into increased hardship, even threatened starvation, for tens of millions of the most vulnerable people.

The developing countries have become part of a wider spiral of contraction which, without remedial action, could drag the countries in the world economy from recession to trade sanctions, withdrawals of credit, competitive devaluations and mutually imposed loss of output far in excess of the restraints many of them have, often prudently, placed on themselves, or, less voluntarily, had thrust upon them.

Finance and trade

Such a contraction is the start of the descent from recession to depression, which shows little sign of being halted. That descent is likely to be hastened by the growing and related difficulties in the world's financial and trading systems. Recession may precipitate a *financial* crisis by creating severe difficulties for commercial banks. When times are hard, companies facing trading losses cannot find bridging finance to wait for better conditions. The weakest go down first. A financial crisis might be defined as the point when the liquidity squeeze on banks becomes itself a force in the recession, transmitted to the productive economy. The banks begin to deny loans to essentially viable borrowers. This has begun to happen. In the US alone, several thousand companies and thirty-five banks had failed in the first ten months of 1982 – the largest number of bankruptcies since the Great Depression. The liquidity squeeze is affecting countries as well as companies – countries with well-managed economies as well as those whose problems are partly self-inflicted.

In 1981 and 1982 the large debts of several East European and developing countries began to prove unmanageable. Some of them have already sought international help. Major corporations too have been forced to call for government assistance. The possibility that other countries could follow, when combined with a number of insolvencies of large and small businesses, threatened to place heavy burdens not only on banks but on national and international financial institutions – burdens which they might be unable to sustain.

At the same time the stagnation of world trade and an increasing disregard for its internationally agreed rules brought other reminders of the 1930s. While world leaders spoke out against protectionism, national politicians called more and more often for protective measures. The European Community was adamant in its unwillingness to contemplate changes in its trade protection. Over its subsidies for agricultural exports, the Community was directly threatened with retaliation by the United States. At the end of 1982, an avalanche of bills for protective measures were before the US Congress. Europe and America complained about trade restrictions in Japan. Perhaps only the fear of retaliation stood between an already deplorable situation and the outbreak of complete anarchy in the trading system.

For the developing countries, the connections between trade and finance made economic management peculiarly difficult. Without adequate finance, imports cannot be paid for; without essential imports, production and exports decline; and without adequate exports, countries are not sufficiently creditworthy to borrow and cannot service their debts. The combined grip of inadequate trade and finance on their economies has become devastating.

Corrections necessary and unnecessary
All the makings of a major world-wide depression are in evidence – wanted by no one, but made daily more likely by each agent in the scene who tries to protect himself from trouble. Yet it can be prevented. Much of the adjustment in the world economy has been necessary. The industrial countries had to fight inflation – though not necessarily or uniquely by the means they adopted, or with so little effort to coordinate policies internationally. The developing countries had to restructure their economies to allow for the new realities of oil prices and world trading and financial conditions; but several of these countries also pursued policies which compounded the damage inflicted by external factors.

There is an extreme view in some quarters that developing countries have brought all their problems on themselves, that what they mainly have to do is improve their domestic 'performance'. That is a dangerous and untenable belief. It is true that some developing countries experiencing oil or other commodity booms in the 1970s embarked on ambitious surges of investment (often encouraged by the North as part of the recycling process) which later proved unsustainable. And the syndrome of overvalued exchange rates, lack of appropriate price and other production incentives (especially for exports and for agriculture), and lax credit policies with double- or even treble-digit inflation, can be found in certain countries. Such policies must be corrected. But the unfavourable external environment has exacerbated their problems beyond measure, and is forcing most countries, even many of the well-managed ones, into excessive retrenchment. 'The developing countries', as the World Bank President put it, 'are being battered by global economic forces outside their control.'[3]

Global adjustment

Thus we identify the major defects in the process of global adjustment as the absence of international coordination of policies, especially among the industrial countries; and the combined weaknesses of the financial and trading systems, which have proved inadequate to cope with the consequences of recession. An excessive share of adjustment is being borne by developing countries. Policies have to be found to redress this situation, to ensure that adjustment is accompanied to a far greater extent than hitherto by growth rather than contraction. They must be consistent with political realities. We believe such policies can be found – not without costs, but with benefits overwhelmingly exceeding them. And the costs of inaction would be vastly greater.

The remaining chapters discuss our proposals and the reasons for them. In the rest of this one, we discuss the causes of developing countries' difficulties; their effects on the North; and the recent record of, and national approaches to, international cooperation.

The Decline in the 1980s: the South

Why have most developing countries been so much worse off at the start of the 1980s than they were in the 1970s? The 1970s also saw recession and inflation in the industrial countries, increases in protectionism, strongly adverse terms of trade; and a sharp rise in the price of oil. Most of the oil-exporting countries benefited; some of the oil-importing countries also adjusted well – they received more back from exports to OPEC countries, or aid and workers' remittances from them, than they paid in addtional costs of oil imports. But for many others, the oil price increase was a severe blow, coming on top of increased import prices for food and manufactures; the fall in their export markets made it still worse.

The growth rates of the low-income countries (other than China and India) fell off more than those of the better-off 'middle-income' countries. Among the latter the newly industrialising countries were less hard hit because they were able to keep expanding their exports, especially exports of manufactures. Though markets were not expanding, they increased their penetration. They were also able to borrow heavily in commercial capital markets, at that time at low or negative real rates of interest, and there was a spectacular growth of private borrowing.

Poorer countries, having mainly primary commodities to export, were unable to increase their foreign earnings. They also suffered more from adverse internal factors, most particularly in Sub-Saharan Africa, where annual growth fell off from 4.0 per cent in the 1960s to 2.4 per cent in the 1970s. Many of these countries were affected by war and civil strife; and drought conditions hurt agriculture severely.

Growth rates of selected groups of countries 1960–81 (average annual percentage growth of GDP)

	1960–70	1970–80		1980	1981
Developing countries					
Low-income:					
China and India	4.5	4.9	China –	6.8	3.0
			India –	6.5	5.6
Other low-income	4.4	3.5	Africa –	0.4	2.7
Middle-income:	5.9	5.6		3.5	1.7
Oil importers	5.8	5.6		3.7	1.0
Oil exporters	6.2	5.5		3.0	3.3
High-income oil exporters		8.5		4.5	– 11.3
Industrial countries (other than E. Europe)	5.2	3.2		1.4	1.2
E. European industrial countries (net material product)	n.a.	6.4		2.7	1.8

Source: World Bank, *World Development Report* 1982. ('Low income' is defined as '1980 GNP per person below $410'.)

Offsetting factors
Nevertheless the 1970s could have been even worse for the low-income countries. There were considerable increases in aid – not least OPEC aid, which constituted one quarter of

all Official Development Assistance during 1975-80. Workers' remittances were very substantial and grew rapidly, easing the balance of payments for a few countries. Others benefited from increased IMF loans, and from brief periods of high commodity prices.

The 1980s began so badly for almost all the oil-importing countries because the offsetting factors were so much weaker. The *better-off* could no longer increase their penetration of markets in the industrial world, which were growing slowly and raising new protective barriers. And their commercial borrowing had to slow down drastically, in part because of their growing liquidity problems. The high interest rates they had to pay while debts rose and exports slumped made banks nervous of continued lending at the earlier levels.

The *poorer countries* were especially vulnerable to the collapse of commodity prices. There was little sign of increased aid – on the contrary, while some donors continued to raise aid flows slowly, others cut back. And the reduction by the US of contributions to the International Development Association (IDA) damaged the World Bank's capacity to assist low-income countries. Workers' remittances from the Gulf were no longer growing as before. Even though most of the poorer countries do not borrow much commercial capital they do borrow some; several have been forced into arrears on outstanding payments on imports. In these circumstances high interest rates – which also apply to SDRs and some other IMF instruments – are burdensome to them too.

Balance of payments squeeze
Stagnation in the industrial world and the oil price increase of 1979-80 have thus been hurting developing countries even more acutely than the external shocks of the 1970s. How severe the situation has become can be judged by the Latin American economies, which still averaged a rate of growth of 6.1 per cent in 1979 and 5.7 per cent in 1980. But the GDP of the oil-importing countries of Latin America and the Caribbean fell by 2.5 per cent in 1981,[4] and all the

23

indications are of another fall in 1982. For many of the poorest countries, especially those of Africa, declines were still greater. Thus when population growth is taken into account, incomes per person in most of the Third World have actually fallen.

Some have escaped the worst. A number of East Asian economies have grown quite strongly in the recent past. India, helped by its successful agriculture, which reduced the need for food imports, and a large IMF loan, is growing at a faster rate than its past average performance – its foreign sector, though important, is relatively small. However, India still faces daunting problems; and its exchange reserves have been falling since 1981. China too, with a high degree of self-sufficiency and high investment rates, has weathered the storms relatively well, but also has difficulties to confront on an awe-inspiring scale.

In general, balance of payments constraints have forced most developing countries to put on the brakes, reducing already low growth rates to intolerable levels. The implications are especially harsh for the poorest countries, a number of which already had negligible growth or even falling output in the 1970s. Growth at an even slower rate means no escape from poverty, and increasing instability, which in turn further impairs economic progress. The fall in the price of oil after 1980 has been modest both compared with its preceding rise, and with the loss of export earnings, especially from commodities. Many countries depend on export or import taxes for the budgetary revenues which pay for health services, education or nutrition programmes. New investments to improve agriculture or start new factories are difficult – even existing investments cannot operate at capacity as the economy begins to run out of imported necessities: spare parts for vehicles, essential drugs, even food or fuel. Efforts to develop human resources and combat hunger and disease have to be curtailed.

The Effects on the North

Our Report emphasised the economic links between North and South. In the 1970s the developing countries' imports from the North, partly financed by their commercial borrowing, helped to prevent the recession in the industrial countries from getting worse, sustaining their production and employment. One study described the effect as equivalent to a significant reflation of the West German economy.[5] Today that effect is reversed; the downturn of growth in developing countries deprives Northern exporters of their markets; and the decline in developing countries' imports is accelerating as major countries in Africa and Latin America run short of foreign exchange. Even more dangerous, as we have seen, the plight of these countries threatens the international financial system itself.

The Mexican crisis of the summer of 1982 has given an ample demonstration of the facts of interdependence. The difficulties faced by Mexico's economy posed a serious threat to commercial banks and to private foreign investors. The political and economic consequences to the United States in particular could have been dire. At the end of 1981 American banks had the largest share of bank loans to Mexico – $21 billion out of a total of $57 billion owed by Mexico to foreign banks. The potential consequences of default by Mexico or the failure of a large US bank were too disturbing to contemplate. The cutback in Mexico's imports hurt exports from the US and many other industrial countries. Economic chaos in Mexico could lead to massive migratory pressures in Texas and California. Not surprisingly, the United States played a major part in initiating the swift action that was taken by the Bank for International Settlements, the International Monetary Fund and the central banks of major Western countries, and took additional measures of its own, including a large advance purchase of Mexican oil for the US strategic reserve.

A recent calculation by the Morgan Guaranty Trust Company has suggested the magnitude of the possible effects of the banking crisis.[6] It considers two scenarios, in which bank lending to non-OPEC developing countries either stops growing completely, or slows to 10 per cent growth (both compared with 20 per cent growth): in the latter case OECD countries' economic growth is cut by ½ a per cent; in the former, 1 per cent. Most of this would occur because of the fall in exports from the OECD countries to the non-OPEC Third World, whose economic growth would be cut even more.

Exports of selected Northern economies 1981 (US $ billion)

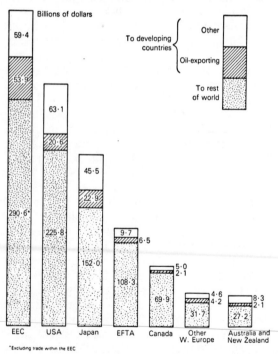

Source: UN *Monthly Bulletin of Statistics*, May/June 1982.

Opposite is a chart showing the exports of the main Western economies to developing countries. The value of these exports to *all* developing countries is considerable, nearly $308 billion in all – over $113 billion for the EEC, nearly $84 billion for the USA, $68 billion for Japan – or over a third of these countries' exports (not counting intra-EEC trade). And the value figures would have been considerably higher had trade in 1981 grown at rates comparable to those of previous years. This trade had been growing rapidly; the 1981 figure for the EEC, for example, actually represented a decline of $4 billion from 1980, compared with growth of an average $15 billion a year in the three previous years. These figures translate into employment – thus 5 per cent of all jobs and *one industrial job in six* in the USA depends on exports to the Third World; in several other countries where trade makes up a higher proportion of total production the figure is even larger. What is at risk for the North is plain to see, if the downward trend of flows of finance and trade with the South is not reversed.

There may still be a few who need convincing that the North will suffer if no action is taken to help the South. But today we do not have the sense that we are addressing an unreceptive audience. It is increasingly obvious that we are all in the same boat, that the North cannot contemplate with unconcern the fact that the South's end of the boat is sinking. The North's end of the boat is already none too buoyant either.

North–South Cooperation 1980-82: Advances and Setbacks

In the first three years of the 1980s, what has been the record of North–South cooperation? Since the Report was published there has only been very modest progress on our Emergency Programme.

● Aid to the poorest countries increased, though not adequately. At the UN Conference on the Least

Developed Countries in 1981, most donors committed themselves to substantial further increases, though the commitments were not precise.

- The IMF expanded its lending considerably, for a time with a more flexible attitude towards conditionality. It also extended its Compensatory Financing Facility to cover cereal imports.
- The World Bank initiated a programme of structural adjustment lending.
- The UN Conference on New and Renewable Sources of Energy agreed on a programme of action in 1981.
- A new Food Aid Convention raised the minimum quantity of food aid from 4.2 to 7.6 million tons, and agreement was reached on replenishing the resources of the International Fund for Agricultural Development, IFAD.

This brief list of items on which some advance took place must be set against the rather longer list of no advance or actual defeat of expectations. That includes the reduction of funds for the International Development Association, IDA, the World Bank's concessional lending arm; the retreat from negotiating an effective International Wheat Agreement; the objection of a number of Northern governments to the sea-bed mining provisions of the Law of the Sea, which so far has prevented their signing the code; worsening trade conditions, including a renewed Multi-Fibre Arrangement more restrictive in application than its predecessor; virtually no progress in any area of commodity trade. And most of the above 'advances' were severely limited:

- After mid-1981 the IMF hardened its lending conditions and a number of credits had to be cancelled in the first half of 1982. There was no new SDR allocation, and the Trust Fund was exhausted. Only towards the end of 1982 did the IMF begin to increase lending again.
- The World Bank's structural adjustment lending remained restricted by its rule that not more than 10

per cent of its loans be used for non-project lending.
- In June 1982 a follow-up to the UN Energy Conference failed to agree on funding or procedures to implement the plan of action.
- At the end of 1982, the United States contribution to IFAD still awaited Congressional legislation, putting in doubt the whole replenishment 'package'.

Strains in the financial system

In September 1982 the world's Finance Ministers and numbers of senior bankers and officials met in Toronto for the Annual Meetings of the World Bank and International Monetary Fund. Many speakers vividly described the problems of their countries and the dangers to the world's financial system.

Yet the results of the meeting were meagre. There was an agreement that the conclusion of negotiations to raise the IMF's quotas should be moved forward to April 1983, though there was no agreement on the size of increase, nor any action on SDR creation despite repeated pleas from the Group of 24, a body representative of developing countries. The United States proposed the setting up of an emergency fund for relief of indebted countries in financial distress. This was greeted with suspicion by many countries since it seemed to be designed to operate selectively and to attempt to bypass the quota issue – which will be discussed further below. But some merits were also noted (not least that it could come into operation faster than quota-related lending), and the Fund's Managing Director made clear that the proposal would be seriously studied. The Executive Board was also asked by the Interim Committee to 'assess the adequacy of existing arrangements to deal with major strains in the international financial system'.

There was also some movement on IDA funding. With the spread of the US commitment over four years instead of three, the possibility of IDA being acutely short of funds in 1984 was real. Since IDA is the principal source of lending for poorer countries – apart from bilateral aid – this was a grave matter. The poorer countries borrow little from commercial banks, but the international recession hurts most of them worse than the better-off nations. In the event arrangements were made to ensure a reasonable level of IDA resources for 1984, largely through an additional commitment from non-US donors which would partially cover the hiatus between the sixth and seventh IDA replenishments caused by the US action.

But altogether the Toronto meeting left countries and banks only modestly, if at all, reassured. A sense of urgency had been conveyed, and the US proposal for an emergency fund had been put on the table. But a clear set of measures to turn the situation round was not identified. While there were reports of serious concern behind the scenes, there was little public recognition by the major industrial countries or the IMF management that any change in the institutions' policies was called for. On the contrary, the usual hymns to the virtues of rigour and discipline were sung with particular fervour.

The world's financial leaders did not see any way out of the international recession and could only resolve on the mixture as before, which was already making things worse rather than better.

The international institutions were in the strange position of advising developing countries to solve their balance of payments deficits by deflation and devaluation, by outward-oriented and export-led strategies, at the same time as the restrictive programmes recommended for both North and South were making it impossible for them to succeed: the recipe might be carried out successfully by any one country; but not by all. If they begin to follow such advice, the result is only to plunge all countries into even greater difficulties.

Under pressure of events, however, the climate of opinion for some movement on finance was changing with remarkable speed by the end of 1982. The possibility of an agreement on IMF quotas even before April 1983 was widely reported, and the US proposal for an emergency fund seemed likely to take the form of an extension of the IMF's General Arrangement to Borrow. But it was far from clear that the various responses would be adequate or satisfactory. And in particular, while it began to seem likely that rescue operations would be mounted for the big borrowers just because they put Northern banks at risk, there was no sign at all of additional initiatives to relieve the plight of poorer countries.

The GATT Ministerial Meeting

The GATT Contracting Parties met at Ministerial level in November 1982 for the first time in nine years. It was, of course, not a 'North–South' occasion, though it had profound implications for developing countries. The background to the meeting was the unfinished business from the Tokyo Round of the Multilateral Trade Negotiations and more importantly the threat posed to the international trading system by the increasing adoption of 'new' protectionist measures, increasing disregard for the GATT rules and disciplines, and growing recognition of the failure of the GATT system to meet new demands on it.

The meeting was able to obtain a 'commitment' to the maintenance of an open trading system; but whether this was strong enough to resist growing domestic pressures for protection in the industrialised countries remains to be seen. The adoption of an improved safeguard system remains postponed; it would have reinforced the commitment to avoid protectionist measures and paved the way for progress in dismantling the panoply of orderly marketing arrangements and voluntary export restraints. Improved procedures have been adopted for dispute settlements; but in other important areas such as agriculture, and textiles and clothing, all that has been achieved is the setting up of studies.

While these studies could no doubt help in providing guidance for progress, the action taken at the GATT Meeting was inadequate in timing and scope in relation to the increasing threat of breakdown of the whole international trading system and the need to ensure expanded trading opportunities for developing countries which would enable them to pay their way and resuscitate their economies. Worst of all what might have been an occasion for a 'ceasefire' on protectionism might do little to prevent an all-out 'trade war' – which no one can win.

Northern approaches

This sorry tale of steps backwards and forwards contrasts strangely with the forthright words of the seven Western heads of government who met in Versailles in June 1982. On North–South cooperation, the Summit communiqué had this to say:

[On trade:]
We are resolved to complete the work of the Tokyo Round and to improve the capacity of the GATT to solve current and future trade problems. We will also work towards the further opening of our markets. We will cooperate with the developing countries to strengthen and improve the multilateral system, and to expand trading opportunities in particular with the newly industrialised countries. We shall participate fully in the forthcoming GATT Ministerial Conference in order to take concrete steps towards these ends.

[On North–South cooperation generally:]
The growth of the developing countries and the deepening of a constructive relationship with them are vital for the political and economic well-being of the whole world. It is therefore important that a high level of financial flows and official assistance should be maintained and that their effectiveness should be increased as far as possible, with responsibilities shared broadly among all countries capable of making a contribution. The launching of global negotiations is a major political objective approved by all participants in the Summit. The latest draft resolution circulated by the Group of 77 is helpful, and the discussion at Versailles showed general acceptance of the view that it would serve as a basis for consultations with the countries concerned. We believe that there is now a good prospect for the early launching and success of the global negotiations, provided that the independence of the Specialised Agencies is guaranteed. At the same time, we are prepared to continue and develop practical cooperation with the developing countries through innovations within the World Bank, through progress in countering instability of commodity

export earnings, through the encouragement of private capital flows, including international arrangements to improve the conditions for private investment, and through a further concentration of official assistance on the poorer countries. This is why we see a need for special temporary arrangements to overcome funding problems for IDA VI, and for an early start to consideration of IDA VII. We will give special encouragement to programmes or arrangements designed to increase food and energy production in developing countries which have to import these essentials, and to programmes to address the implications of population growth.

In the field of balance of payments support, we look forward to progress at the September IMF Annual Meeting towards settling the increase in the size of the Fund appropriate to the coming Eighth Quota Review.

Did the Summit powers mean what they said? They were certainly in no hurry to follow it up. Except for limited moves towards the increasing of IMF resources, little or no progress has been made in these areas. And, both among the seven powers at the Summit and in the industrialised world generally, national approaches to development do not give ground for optimism.

Within the past year, it is true, the EEC Commission formulated some fresh approaches for the European Community's cooperation with developing countries which are imaginative and sensitive to needs. They include improvements to the facilities of the Lomé Convention; new forms of trade and financial cooperation with non-ACP countries; a GNP-related target for aid provided through the Community; and priority action to assist developing countries, especially the poorest, in attaining food self-sufficiency. But these proposals are yet to be welcomed by member countries of the Community and initial signals have not been promising. Indeed, at the recent GATT Ministerial Meeting, Europe's protectionist stand cast a shadow between expectation and performance in the vital area of international trade.

While we expect much from Europe, we do no less from the United States and would look with dismay on the possibility of a new commitment to international development in which the United States does not whole-heartedly join. Yet as anyone reading this document will observe, in a number of areas where there had been progress, the United States in the past months has played a negative role. It has given up its earlier position as a leader of the West in cooperation for development. It still has the world's largest aid programme, but one of the lowest as a proportion of national income. Yet while it has cut back on aid, it has also gone back on commitments of previous administrations in some fields and hindered international accord in others. We strongly believe – as do many Americans – that important United States interests are served by the system of international cooperation: by the multilateral agencies; by the UN family; by bilateral assistance programmes and by the international machinery of consultation on trade and financial matters. We urge the United States in its interests, in all our interests, not to turn away from these cooperative enterprises, but, on the contrary, to act once more in keeping with its size and power as an enlightened leader of the world community.

And there are other industrialised countries like Japan and some of the developed countries outside the European Community that have prosperous economies. Some are among the most progressive of the North in development cooperation; others could do much more. They have declared their interest in intensifying their cooperation with the Third World, and have taken some positive steps in this direction. They should now accelerate the progress of recent years.

The role of the East
And, as in our Report, which aroused some expression of interest in the Soviet Union and Eastern Europe, we again call on these countries to play a more active part in North–South issues. At present there are divisions in the West – fundamentally, divisions over whether closer economic ties between East and West will lead ultimately to a lessening of international tensions, or whether the West

should try to influence the East's policies by inflicting economic penalties on them when displeased with their actions, or by tying increases in economic cooperation to cooperation over other issues. As long as this debate is unresolved, progress on many matters close to our preoccupations – not least that of disarmament – will be difficult. But at certain points in the present document we observe that East European countries should assume a more significant role in international discussions – on trade and finance, and perhaps most particularly on energy and on food where they have a strong interest. We also urge them to expand their aid and trade with the Third World, which are presently modest. We are well aware of all the familiar obstacles. Yet the desirable objectives of world development cannot be attained if a large section of the industrial world continues forever to pursue a separate path.

Political Dangers

So far we have referred only to economic interests which are shared by North and South. Yet they also share strong political interests in the proposals we put forward.

These political interests are based on the fact that development – widely shared development – is a condition for national and international stability. Some would argue that the major sources of international conflict do not have their origins in poverty but rather in such things as East–West tensions, conflict in the Middle East or Southern Africa, rebel movements, territorial claims. But such views only take the argument half-way. While many causes underlie conflict and instability, failure of development often provides the conditions in which they can originate and flourish. Indeed the President of the United States recognised this in recommending his 'Caribbean Basin Initiative' to Congress: he said the countries concerned were faced with 'economic disaster', and the region's economic misery 'would be exploited by extremist groups'. Yet even this 'Initiative' remains a promise.

35

Financial and economic crises that lead to weak or falling governments are often the result of inadequate or inequitable development. In the political vacuum which may thus result a country can become vulnerable to outside interference, which then contributes, as the Report said, to East–West tensions. Who is to say whether the recent history of Afghanistan might not have been very different if its development had produced a strong economy and a viable government capable of resisting outside interference? Yet in the decade before the Soviet intervention it was one of the lowest aid recipients for its size and poverty.

Certainly the situations of that country and many others now call forth military expenditures well in excess of anything that was ever provided to promote their development – development which might have forestalled political crisis. There was a time when aid was seen as a competition for the allegiance of developing countries between the major powers of East and West. Commission members did not and would not endorse a return to anything resembling that competition. But we do see one of the main purposes of development – and of international cooperation for development – as the creation of nation states capable of sustaining their own political independence. That is among the essential foundations of international stability.

The example of drugs

One example of the dangers of the failure of development is drugs. Of course the problem has many dimensions of which the criminal element is much the most significant and the most dangerous. But as far as supply is concerned, the poverty of rural areas of one or two Asian and Latin American countries is a key factor. Thousands of people in such areas turn to growing the plant sources of cocaine, marijuana or opium for want of alternative livelihoods – even when cultivation of these plants is illegal. Once again it is a situation where neglect leads to the costs of 'cure' being many times those of prevention – the costs, before remedial action is taken, being reckoned in crime, corruption, violent death and ruined lives. The need is now for measures of control. But the only real remedy at the supply end is for poor people to have better ways to make a living. The international economy plays its part too – for one or two countries exports of these substances bulk very large in foreign exchange earnings and are difficult to replace. We spoke of this subject in the Report. The situation has become much worse. Once again the message is that the consequences of failure of development can spread far beyond the areas where that failure occurs; and that the resources for development which would have prevented the problem from becoming so serious are but a fraction of those needed to cope with it once it emerges.

Equity and stability
The origins of political instability are indeed highly complex and economic development cannot be guaranteed to eliminate it. In fact highly unequal development, development which creates and defeats new expectations, or passes by significant sections of a country's population, can foster instability. But development which relieves men and women from the indignity of poverty, which replaces social deprivation with social justice, will work in the opposite direction. Supporting equitable development is both morally preferable to and less expensive than the military and other measures its absence may make necessary.

Disarmament
Another aspect – and a grave one – of the worsening of the international environment during the last three years has been the increase in arms production and expenditure. We refer to the economic role of armaments in the next chapter. But the complete failure of the UN Special Session on Disarmament in the summer of 1982 was one of the most dispiriting of recent events. In 1980 we spoke of world military expenditure of $450 billion. By 1982 it was $650 billion. *what sort of increase in real terms?*
Our Report went into some of the questions of
Corrected for inflation?, depreciation? 37

armaments and the relation of disarmament and development. Since it came out, there have appeared the excellent reports of the United Nations Expert Group on Disarmament and Development and *Common Security*, the Report of the Palme Commission on Disarmament and Security Issues. The latter deals with technical aspects of disarmament and its global political setting, including a number of valuable proposals bearing specifically on Third World security.

It is beyond the scope of the present document to enter into these issues in detail. All we can do is to add our plea to theirs: that genuine disarmament be pursued as the first priority of international action, to rid the world both of the growing insecurity of the proliferation of weapons, and of their unacceptable costs, which now pose a serious threat to several industrial and developing economies.

2 Finance

The prolonged recession in the industrialised countries of the North is at the root of the crisis in the world economy. Its devastating impact on the South comes on top of an accumulation of serious and unresolved development problems. The drastic loss of import purchasing power these countries have now suffered feeds back into further losses of exports and jobs in the industrialised countries.

For the South, the consequential financial distress is causing cutbacks on imports, on investment, on development programmes, on growth. But every country's retrenchment makes other countries' tasks more difficult. World recovery is essential to reverse that process. But until recovery begins, and to help it begin, there are financial initiatives which can prevent excessive retrenchment and diminish both the threats posed to developing countries' growth, to world trade and the trading system, and the acute dangers to the banks and financial markets.

The immediate financial problems of the banks should never be allowed to conceal the more fundamental political consequences in countries which face severe contraction and lower living standards as a result of their losses of foreign exchange and debt burdens. Any new loans on market terms, whether from the commercial banks, national governments, or the IMF, can help to alleviate the immediate crisis but will only increase these countries' indebtedness. Only a major recovery of the world economy and measures to ease debt service burdens could alleviate the situation. Prolonged and excessively severe measures to

loans to ease hard times only cause more indebtedness

ensure debt repayments can be ultimately counter-productive, leading to growing social unrest, impossible strains on governments and prospects of revolution or chaos.

Cooperation for Expansion

There is no way of averting a slide into depression or of moving the world economy on to a path of recovery without bold measures to shore up the international financial system. However, even this will not be enough unless the industrialised countries turn from their preoccupation with inflation, budgetary deficits, and balance of payments problems – which are themselves a result of the stagnation in world trade and pro-duction – and strive instead for resumed growth.

No country can pull itself out of its present economic plight merely by its own efforts. So much production and investment are today directed towards markets in other countries that domestic policies cannot offset the contraction in income and employment that is due to recession and instability in world markets. But so far there has been no move towards concerted expansion, and the way forward is not easy to determine.

As the Bank for International Settlements has put it, 'Between the Scylla of a renewed acceleration of inflation and the Charybdis of protracted stagnation, the path looks extremely narrow.'[7] Yet that path must be found. At the end of 1982 it appeared that major industrial countries were at last moving away from the policy of squeezing inflation out of the economy at any cost. The costs were staggering, with unemployment rates of 14 per cent in some European countries and over 10 per cent in the United States.

Some of the lessening of inflation came from low commodity and energy prices which could only last in the conditions of recession. There was no guarantee either that, without new policies, low wage settlements would continue once stronger economic activity resumed. For some countries exchange rates were too high for recovery; but their reduction too would bring at least a temporary increase of inflation. On the other hand, growth itself could bring reductions in inflation, through an improved fiscal balance, and through reduced unit costs at higher levels of output. But the old policies were failing; they appeared to contain *no* path between 'acceleration of inflation and protracted stagnation', as well as menacing acute dangers to the financial system, to trade, to long-run industrial health, and to the developing countries.

Will the path be found, or will a choice have to be made between continued, possibly worsening, recession, or growth with modest inflation? Certainly the dangers of depression now greatly outweigh those of inflation. The time has come to move on the path to growth. There are no quick solutions. All are agreed that the past high rates of inflation were intolerable, that excessive expansion has to be avoided. But growth requires investment, and investment not just lower interest rates but the prospect of rising demand. And the scale of investment required is very large if declines of productivity are to be reversed, more employment created, and the North continue its own adjustment to changes in patterns of world production and competition.

The countries in trade surplus, Japan and Germany, and the United States, for whom trade is a smaller part of the economy, have the greatest freedom of action; for the others, balance of payments constraints will constrict individual efforts of expansion unless there is a more or less simultaneous resumption of growth. There will in any case be changes in current accounts as growth is resumed. To smooth the way for joint economic expansion there should be general agreement to finance without hesitation such growth-induced deficits.

Interest and exchange rates
In October 1982 the US Federal Reserve Board announced a change of monetary policy which permitted a decline of interest rates. It is a salutary reminder of the limits of

international cooperation; the US had been pressed to take such a course for many months. There is machinery for coordination in the industrial North, most particularly at official level in the OECD's 'Working Party III' and its Economic Policy Committee. The difficulties into which the North has fallen through failures of consultation must lead to the machinery's being more productively used. It could be disastrous if there were a return to tighter money and higher interest rates. This issue and other *key elements of monetary and fiscal policy should now be under urgent cooperative review by governments and central banks so that an appropriate pace of expansion can be agreed on and set in motion*, and a better relation among exchange rates be maintained than has recently prevailed.

In recent years wide swings in the exchange rates of the US dollar, the Japanese yen, the pound sterling and the Deutschmark have added to financial insecurity. A 'high' exchange rate makes a country's imports cheap and can lead to demands for protection and subsidies; a 'low' one creates pressures in other countries for discrimination and retaliatory measures. Exchange rates which bore little relation to countries' competitiveness undoubtedly contributed to the distortions of the trading system in recent years.

High interest rates in some countries have forced others to choose between exchange rate depreciation and imported inflation, or a domestic interest rate higher than desirable for sustaining the level of economic activity and credit expansion. The variability of exchange rates has also contributed to uncertainty for investment and foreign trade.

While few would desire a return to the fixed-rate regimes of earlier times, many would welcome the confinement of fluctuations at least within agreed bounds, and intervention to keep relationships between currencies inside those bounds when they seem likely to depart from their appropriateness to fundamental economic conditions. This would be an important component of needed improvements in the world economy. It requires both policy coordination among the industrial countries and possible intervention. In fact the five countries whose currencies are represented in the SDR have been asked to report on the need for intervention at the IMF meeting due early in 1983. *We would strongly support action to provide greater stability to relationships among exchange rates.*

With stronger international cooperation, we are confident that the path to recovery through financial and monetary expansion can be found. To those who fear that it is too dangerous to attempt in the light of possible inflationary consequences, we would point to the far greater dangers of not making the attempt. The case can hardly be better put than in the words of Mr H. J. Witteveen, former Managing Director of the IMF:

With present high unemployment rates and low capacity utilisation, surpluses in oil and other raw material markets and pervasive deflationary tendencies in the world financial system, the risk that a somewhat higher increase in the money supply would rekindle inflation is practically non-existent. This should be explained clearly and forcefully to overcome dogmatic and unrealistic monetarist fears. The danger that recession and disinflation will turn into deflation and lead to a world depression has become so great that the time has come for some shift in policy priorities from fighting inflation to preventing depression.[8]

Arms spending and recovery: a common error
We cannot leave the issue of the North's recovery without warning against a common error. One of the tragic developments of the last three years has been the rise in arms spending. Some think that this will help the world out of recession. In fact military expenditure is very much more a part of the world's economic problem than its solution. At any given level of public expenditure, the higher the proportion of spending devoted to weapons procurement, the smaller the amount of employment created. Military expenditure may also be more inflationary than other public spending. The alleged benefit of technological spin-off is also fallacious; technological advance can be promoted directly with far greater economy.

43

There is no lack of political support for other forms of public expenditure: on the contrary, the public of the industrial North frequently complains of the cuts in social and infrastructure investment. It cannot be argued that these economies require high levels of military expenditure for any economic purpose. And high military expenditure is an obstacle to the pursuit of all those objectives which affect their national security and to which military measures are not relevant: those objectives include the development of the Third World.

The South: deficits and debts

Falling export earnings together with high oil prices and interest rates have wrought havoc in the economies of developing countries in the last three years. The overall current account deficits of oil-importing countries (excluding official transfers) rose from $44 billion in 1979 to $73 billion in 1980 and $88 billion in 1981. The increase would have been still greater had finance been available.

Oil accounted for an average 25 per cent of their imports – in many countries very much more – having grown from about 6 per cent in the 1960s. Interest payments for all developing countries rose to $51 billion in 1981. They were expected to exceed $56 billion in 1982, more than double the 1979 level – most of it due to interest rate increases, since debt outstanding less than doubled.

Speaking in April 1982, the Managing Director of the IMF said: 'The external deficits of the developing countries have reached record levels. Of those that are net importers of oil, half now face current account deficits of 12 per cent of gross domestic product or more – about three times their level of a decade ago. Deficits of this magnitude clearly cannot be sustained in terms of future debt service capacity. In 1981, the ratio of debt service payments to exports of goods and services for the non-oil developing countries had risen to about 20 per cent – compared with 17 per cent in 1978. What is more, the debt service ratio for the low-income developing countries has been rising faster than the average.'[9] The Managing

Director was not speaking of short-term debt, which raises debt service ratios still further – see below. And since he spoke, the situation has worsened.

Debt is the result of borrowing, and developing countries' debt should not in itself be regarded as something undesirable. It is undesirable when borrowed capital is not adequately used to enhance productive capacity, or when the average terms of debt are not commensurate with the borrower's capacity to repay, and lenders fight shy of lending more. The latter has been the experience of several countries. Total foreign indebtedness of developing countries reached some $630 billion by the end of 1981. It consisted of $490 billion of medium- or long-term debt, and $140 billion of short-term debt (that is, of maturities of less than one year). Of those sums, about half was owed to commercial banks – virtually all the short-term debt, and more than a third of the rest. ('The rest' is made up largely of debts owed to official lenders – governments and international institutions – other private borrowing, and export credits which are also owed to commercial banks but are guaranteed by official agencies.)

In the five years 1976-81 total debt grew by 20 per cent a year (it was $251 billion in 1976). But the part owed to banks grew by 25 per cent a year, and the short-term part grew fastest of all, 29 per cent a year. In the early 1980s the combination of rocketing interest rates and bunching of maturities has put a number of countries into a position of very high obligations. They can pay them from net foreign earnings or by drawing down reserves. But developing country reserves have fallen rapidly. And in trade they have had net deficits, not net earnings. The only way they can meet their debt obligations is by borrowing more.

The countries with most of this high interest debt are the better-off developing countries. Most developing countries are in deficit on the current account of their balance of payments. The low-income countries' borrowing is mostly on a concessional basis: thus their capacity to grow depends crucially on aid. The better-off borrow from official and private sources. As far as their commercial debt is concerned, they would usually expect to reschedule any part that they could not pay. This mainly means that banks have effectively to extend the maturity of their loans, or lend countries more in order to be repaid on what is due now. Until recently they were quite willing to do this; it was profitable for them, and their borrowers – for the most part – looked sound.

The situation has in fact been growing shakier ever since 1979, but the deterioration has accelerated since 1981. For the borrowers there was a growing liquidity or cash-flow problem. More and more countries were seeking official debt-reschedulings through the 'Paris Club' and elsewhere. The banks looked at these events, at the worsening current-account position of developing countries, and at their own balance sheets and their exposure in these countries. They had other problems too. Poland had a large amount of bank debt which had to be rescheduled after the economic and political crisis of 1981. Big corporate borrowers were in trouble in the North.

When Mexico, the biggest single Southern borrower from the banks, had to seek help internationally in the summer of 1982, few bankers felt any longer that the financial system was secure. Other very large commercial borrowers were grappling with their financial burdens, uncertain of success: Brazil, Argentina, Yugoslavia, Korea. The IMF had substantial resources to assist any normal number of smaller countries; but it would be stretched to take in both those and any of the bigger borrowers who might eventually call on it. By late 1982 Argentina, Brazil, Chile, Ecuador, Mexico, Nigeria, the Philippines and South Africa had all approached the Fund for large amounts.

Bank lending to the South
Now a debate has begun about the wisdom of the large volume of sovereign lending by commercial banks. They have been accused of irresponsibility, and the borrowers of profligacy. We would not be so harsh. Some banks have

been imprudent in their exposure in certain countries; some borrowers have used some of the capital for investments with very low returns. But the fault in the great bulk of the borrowing and lending lay mainly in a failure to anticipate the conjunction of circumstances which has made the resulting debt unmanageable: high interest rates and the lengthening and deepening of the recession, and all they have done to damage the borrowers' foreign exchange position. It was a failure to assess correctly what statisticians call the 'downside risk'.

Before the criticism became widespread, the banking system had been congratulated – not least by itself – for having satisfactorily managed the 'recycling' of OPEC surpluses. The weaknesses of leaving so much to the market were apparent, especially in its 'herd behaviour' – the tendency for many banks to follow a few leading banks, with a resulting potential for volatility in flows. We argued, as did many others, that it would have been safer for a larger proportion of those flows to be channelled through public institutions with governmental support.[10] But for the most part borrowers, lenders and the world economy in general benefited from the high levels of activity which the flows permitted. It is essential that private flows continue, with support from international institutions and central banks, albeit with appropriate adjustments on all sides.

Bank debt
The following charts illustrate some of the magnitudes in greater detail. The first shows the bank debt of the four biggest developing country borrowers from commercial banks, the second that of selected East European countries. They give some sense of the magnitudes involved. Even more revealing are the figures for individual banks in particular countries: the four US banks with the largest exposure in Mexico were owed individually amounts between $1.4 and $2.5 billion at end-1981. These sums, though only a very small percentage of their total assets, were equivalent to anywhere between 40 and 60 per

Bank Debt of Selected Developing Countries, End of Year 1981

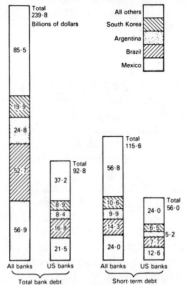

Sources: Carron, 1982; Bank for International Settlements;
Federal Financial Institutions Examination Council.

Bank Debt of East European Countries, End of Year 1981

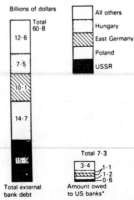

*Total amounts owed to US banks after adjustments
for guarantees and external borrowing.

Sources: Carron, 1982; Bank for International Settlements;
Federal Financial Institutions Examination Council.

cent of their capital. (Capital/asset ratios were of the order of one to twenty or twenty-five.)

By late 1982 it was obvious that something must be done. 'Credit', as one banker put it, 'is suspicion asleep.'[11] But suspicion was becoming unease, if not anxiety. Bank lending to developing countries slowed down sharply. The world economy was already approaching a financial crisis, in the sense defined in Chapter 1, that funds began to be in short supply even for technically sound borrowers. But the possibilities of worse, of a financial collapse, were being quite openly talked about. The financial distress of the Third World had become distressing to the North.

Low-income countries
Most of the discussion of bank debt is particularly relevant to the problems of the middle-income countries which borrow most heavily in commercial markets. But the poorer countries are in many ways worse off still. As already noted, their growth – with some exceptions – fell off more than that of the better-off countries in the 1970s, several of them experiencing prolonged economic decline. Now in the early 1980s their plight is acute. It is they who are most vulnerable to the disastrous falls in commodity prices. They have little foreign exchange for needed capital goods or other essentials of development. Many countries cannot even afford vital imports of food, fuel, spare parts or medicines; existing productive capacity is under-utilised, and transport and health systems suffer. They live a precarious financial existence, seeking short-term credits for day-to-day imports; increasing numbers of countries are falling into arrears on current import payments.

The problems of external balance directly affect governments' budgets, since for many governments, import duties and export taxes are a major source of revenue. And a contracting economy pressurises the budget even further. The threat of financial disaster and political and economic chaos and misery now stares several of the poorest countries in the face. For a few it has already arrived. We are profoundly concerned that the needs of many countries – and not just the poorest – are being ignored because Western banks are not much involved in their fate. That state of affairs must not be allowed to continue.

Proposals

Our financial proposals are of various kinds. International agencies can lend more themselves; they can provide for the contingencies which look so threatening today. The International Monetary Fund must enlarge its role, with new SDR issues, lending from increased quotas, and from other borrowing. The World Bank group and bilateral donors must expand their assistance. If these things are done, the flow of private lending can expand, provided that the rest of the international environment is supportive. It is essential that banks increase their lending to developing countries. For the poorer countries, there are no alternatives to increased aid – though that is not all that is necessary; reforms of aid policy are also required.

The International Monetary Fund
The International Monetary Fund was established partly with a view to avoiding the experience of the 1930s, when the international repercussions of national policies did so much to extend the damage of the depression. The Fund would assist international cooperation in the monetary field, promote exchange rate stability and the growth of liberal international trade, and provide financial support and cooperation to its members in balance of payments difficulties. It is often forgotten that its Articles enjoin the IMF to carry out the last of these functions in a manner that will not harm national or international prosperity. High levels of employment, income and economic development are, the Articles said, 'the primary objectives of economic policy'.

Countries seek assistance from the IMF mainly for balance of payments adjustment. But the IMF's treatment of adjustment in recent years seems to have lost sight of the 'primary objectives'. The world situation now calls for a substantial enlargement of the Fund's role and its resources. This must go hand in hand with changes in its adjustment policies or 'conditionality' – changes which we regard as fully consistent with the Fund's accepted functions.

Why the Fund must be enlarged
The enlargement of the Fund's resources is necessary to restore its proper role in providing balance of payments support, and relieving the shortage of reserves and liquidity affecting many countries. Expanded IMF lending will permit countries having to adjust a greater possibility of doing so without damaging their prospects for growth. It is also essential for the Fund to have additional borrowing powers to cope with emergency situations. The measures for these purposes have already been under discussion: the eighth quota increase, extension of the General Arrangements to Borrow, SDR allocations, borrowing from Central Banks and possibly other sources. But we do not believe the international community is seized with the magnitude and the gravity of the problem. The size of changes that were being contemplated at the end of 1982 was inadequate, and a new perspective is urgently required.

Quotas   What exactly are quotas?
IMF quotas at end-1982 stood at the equivalent of SDR 61 billion. Only part of the quota subscriptions are freely usable by the Fund; these constitute the Fund's primary resources. The Fund has borrowed in the past to supplement these 'ordinary resources', but has borrowed more substantial amounts recently to finance its policy of enlarged access, as its ordinary resources would not have been capable of meeting the demands made upon it. *The number and scale of likely demands in the circumstances of the 1980s are such as to justify at least a doubling of quotas.* It was reported in December 1982 that agreement

51

was near among the Group of Ten industrialised countries for a quota increase of about 50 per cent. But in our view such an increase is inadequate for three sets of reasons.

The first relate to the principle that the Fund should pursue a policy of prudence and sound finance; it should at all times cover its lending commitments with its ordinary resources or with lines of credit arranged for the purpose. In financing standby and extended arrangements the Fund uses a mixture of ordinary and borrowed resources, but for the remainder of its facilities it relies on its ordinary resources. The Fund's net uncommitted ordinary resources have already been depleted considerably and, on the basis of projected commitments over the next eighteen months, could well be below SDR 10 billion by early 1984. This would be only a fifth of members' total reserve positions in the Fund. A 50-per-cent increase in quotas would do no more than boost this liquidity ratio to between a half and two thirds, which is still low in relation to past levels. There would thus be a need for considerable additional borrowings even after quota increases become effective, which runs counter to the view of the Interim Committee that quotas should provide the principal source of Fund resources.

The second set of reasons relate to the changes that we are suggesting for access to the Fund's facilities, especially the Compensatory Financing Facility (CFF). This facility at present supports only half of the total export shortfalls of countries approaching the Fund for assistance even on the insufficient basis of the quota limits and calculation of shortfalls employed by the Fund. If our proposals below are accepted, drawings under the CFF could triple. This together with other expansion would only be made possible by a minimum increase of 100 per cent in quotas.

The final set of reasons relate to the decline in the magnitude of quotas in relation to other indicators of world activity. For example, even if quotas were doubled, they would only equal 5 per cent of world imports by 1984-5, restoring the ratio of ten years earlier, and still considerably below the 9 per cent of 1970 or 12 per cent of 1965.

Quotas do not require budgetary allocations, and the bulk is paid most commonly in the form of promissory notes in a country's own currency, drawn on its central bank. But they do require legislation; thus even after agreement is reached on the size of the quota increase, it takes many months before lending on the basis of the enlarged quotas can begin. Because very large borrowings may be called for in the near future to assist heavily indebted countries, the creation of additional borrowing authority is urgent

Additional borrowing

The US 'safety net' proposal discussed in Toronto is now being discussed in terms of an enlargement of the Fund's General Arrangements to Borrow or GAB. Under the GAB the Group of Ten industrial countries provide credit to the Fund for financing large drawings to 'forestall or cope with an impairment of the international monetary system'. Hitherto it has been confined to lending among these countries, and has been used to supplement IMF resources for use under its normal facilities. If the GAB is to be used as a 'safety net' for developing countries in critical situations, it would have to be altered to permit lending to these countries and – if it is to operate rapidly – under new modalities of lending.

But if it is financed by the Group of Ten, and they control its operations, it will provide resources to countries selected at their discretion, rather than making the desired expansion of Fund lending available to all members. It cannot be regarded as a satisfactory alternative to a share of the proposed quota increase. Such an expansion of the GAB should therefore be separate from and additional to the doubling of quotas. It lies within the power of the Group of Ten, however, to begin lending swiftly from this facility to countries in need and not wait for further emergencies.

We also support further means of maintaining capital flows at an adequate level in the near term. One is that *the Fund should continue to borrow from central banks to augment its resources, and also borrow in capital markets.* This will be facilitated by the knowledge of an adequate agreed quota increase. Secondly *the bridge-financing operations of the Bank for International Settlements should be expanded*, especially for the periods between a country's applying for Fund credits and its receiving the first disbursements. For this purpose governments of developed countries should encourage their central banks to provide additional short-term deposits to the BIS.

A possible objection?

In the discussion of central banks' functions below, we share the views of those who do not wish to have made too clear what action central banks would take if the financial system were in trouble, in order that banks should in no way *rely* on the prospect of rescue when making their assessments of acceptable and unacceptable risk in their operations. Does not the proposal for emergency borrowing authority under discussion in the Fund violate this principle? We believe not, providing two points are kept in mind.

Firstly, this proposal is designed to cope with the critical and extraordinary situations *already reached* by a small number of heavily indebted countries, which could in imaginable circumstances overwhelm the Fund and the international financial system if no contingency arrangements exist. There are many ways in which the proposal could be designed to prevent it from encouraging imprudent behaviour in the future.

Secondly, an important feature must be built into the proposal, namely that where commercial borrowers are concerned, a very substantial proportion of the finance made available in association with the IMF should be provided by the commercial banks themselves, albeit in part under some form of co-financing or guarantees or other arrangements with the institutions, industrial country governments and the borrowing countries. Banks must continue to extend new credits and reschedule existing ones. There must not be a major substitution of public funds for the banks' lending. The borrowing countries will have to undergo necessary adjustments. But the banks which have steered into these waters must be lashed to the wheel in the storm, not allowed to go below and sleep.

The $85 billion gap

But even if the above measures were taken, the response would still be wholly inadequate to meet the dimensions of the problem. For in 1981 world reserves declined by $200 billion,[12] and at the end of that year reserves of developing countries were down to a total of $106 billion, or two and a half months' imports. In Africa, they could have financed less than one month's. In 1982 they have dropped still further. (Of the thirty-two countries in payments arrears at the end of 1981, twenty were in Africa.) Most critical of all, in the past two years taken together developing countries have lost something close to $85 billion of foreign exchange which would otherwise have been available for imports; similarly, and as a result, the industrial countries' exports to them have undergone a huge decline.

Specifically, between 1980 and 1982, developing countries' export revenues fell by $40 billion; their debt service payments rose by $37 billion;[13] and long- and medium-term lending fell by $5–10 billion.[14] The principal offset to that was an increase of short-term borrowing, by approximately $25 billion a year on average in the last four years – but this is mainly used for refinancing debt service, and is highly undesirable in itself, piling up problems for the future.

For something approaching a restoration of developing countries' import capacity to 1980 levels – which were themselves already creating difficulties – resources comparable to this $85 billion fall would be needed. Where are these to come from?

The IMF quota increase will not make new lending possible before 1984. But assuming the IMF borrowed on a scale that would give it comparable resources in 1983, it could lend an additional $10–11 billion. Depending on the scale of the GAB increase and the rate at which lending would flow from it, a comparable amount might be available from that source. The recommendation below on World Bank programme lending could increase immediate capital flows by perhaps $2 billion or more. None of the other financial proposals mean significant additional new medium- or long-term lending in 1983.

Few people imagine OECD growth in 1983 will add very substantially to recent levels of developing countries' export earnings. Every one-per-cent decline in interest rates saves developing countries $2 billion of debt service, and we hope they will decline further. As for private lending, it would be unrealistic to expect any major recovery in 1983. Even if all these three factors contribute more than seems likely, it is quite evident that of the $85 billion foreign exchange loss referred to, a vast amount, at least half, is not going to be restored unless additional measures are taken.

The need for a major SDR allocation
There is an inescapable case, therefore, for a major new allocation of SDRs or Special Drawing Rights. A large injection of liquidity is needed merely to prevent the international economy from contracting further. The time has come when the emphasis must shift to averting depression. There is need also, therefore, to provide a major new impulse to recovery. The latest *Annual Report* of the Bank for International Settlements cites the 'contraction of international liquidity' in the early 1980s as one of 'those factors which could impede the orderly resumption of economic growth or depress the world economy even further'.

We have shown that even a doubling of quotas, borrowing by the Fund and new lines of credit through the GAB of the order contemplated are grossly inadequate. Moreover, these arrangements would take time to implement and their conditional access would require time to agree stabilisation programmes with the Fund. *We are convinced that present circumstances demand the use of SDRs. The level must be very large and related to the extent of the declines in international liquidity and the level of deficits which must be financed if contractionary forces are to be reversed.*

In light of the deepening recession, the considerable reduction in inflation, the severe reduction in international liquidity, and the rapid deterioration in the international financial situation, we believe that arguments about the inflationary consequences of SDR allocations have lost relevance. Article XVIII of the IMF's Articles of Agreement provides that in SDR decisions the IMF 'shall seek in meeting the long-term global need to supplement existing reserve assets in such a manner as . . . will avoid economic stagnation and deflation as well as excess demand and inflation in the world'. The conditions for a major issue of SDRs are satisfied today.

Besides the quick provision of relief, an SDR allocation has other advantages at this time. SDRs have declined considerably as a proportion of non-gold reserves. An allocation of about SDR 10–12 billion per year for the next three years is required merely to restore this ratio to about the level it held after the first period of allocation which ended in 1972. A further advantage is that SDR allocations do not create repayment obligations, a particularly important feature. However, for the poorest countries, subsidised interest rates would be required to facilitate SDR use.

In light of the circumstances which necessitate a large allocation, there is a strong case for a distribution which would reflect the needs of the poorest countries and of the monetary system as a whole. A larger proportion than in the past would have to go to developing countries. The simplest way to achieve this without amendment of the IMF's Articles would be if those industrial countries in a position to do so were to relinquish at least in part their share of the new allocation. The greater the amount thus obtained for the use of developing countries, the smaller the total allocation need be.

In any case, the new allocation of SDRs will have to be very substantial. This will give the SDR a somewhat larger significance in the international monetary system in keeping with objectives already agreed in the Fund. At a later stage, a review of the Bretton Woods system which cannot now be long deferred would provide opportunity to consider ways in which the role of the SDR could be further strengthened. For the present, however, an essential need in bringing about world economic recovery is a major emergency issue of SDRs.

Use of the Fund's enlarged resources
Increase in the Fund's resources would permit a welcome increase in drawings under all the Fund's facilities. Our particular interest focuses first on two among them, the Extended Fund Facility and the Compensatory Financing Facility.

Up to the mid-1970s payments deficits were broadly classified into three categories: temporary, due to climatic or cyclical factors which could be expected to be self-correcting and not calling for adjustment by the country concerned; those due to excess demand, caused by over-expansion in domestic monetary or fiscal policy, which had to be corrected; and fundamental disequilibria which would exist even without excess demand, for which exchange rate adjustments and other measures were needed.

The Extended Fund Facility
Financing could be needed for deficits of any of these

kinds. Countries have access to Fund resources both of 'low' and 'high' conditionality. The 'first credit tranche' of low conditionality applies largely to measures countries would take on their own with minimum Fund supervision. Temporary, self-correcting deficits would mainly be financed at low conditionality under the compensatory facility. Higher conditionality is attached to the upper credit tranches needed for the other types of deficits under the Fund's twelve-month standby arrangements.

In the mid-1970s a further kind of payments deficit in addition to these three began to be recognised: where a country needs a significant adjustment of production to confront a change in the external environment that is *not* expected to be temporary, such as that caused by the rise in oil prices and all the circumstances surrounding it. If the country cannot achieve the turn-around required in imports and exports in a short period of time, by demand management or devaluation, then it must effect a change in the structure of production, substituting domestic production for imports and generating more goods for export. The Extended Fund Facility (EFF) was introduced in 1974 with such structural adjustment in mind. It permits three-year programmes, with repayment over a maximum of ten years (compared with a maximum of five years under other facilities).

A recent study from the Institute for International Economics[15] has observed that the terms of reference of the EFF do not completely cover the case of structural adjustment in the sense defined, as being required to meet permanent changes in the external environment which necessitate time-consuming alterations in the structure of a country's domestic productive activities. The study recommended that the official description of the purposes of the EFF be reformulated 'in order to specify its role as that of aiding a country to adjust to a structural deficit' in this sense. We endorse this proposal, and urge the full resumption of EFF lending for this purpose.

Compensatory finance

The Commission's Report proposed an increase in the size and coverage of the Compensatory Financing Facility (CFF), which was originally designed to compensate for export shortfalls beyond a country's control. We repeat the proposal now. The coverage has been extended, since we wrote, to cereal imports but not to other temporary causes of deficits, as we proposed, including movements in import prices which have become vastly more significant since the CFF was set up. The CFF has become increasingly important: it accounted for a third of all IMF drawings in 1981, and looked likely to exceed that proportion in 1982. This form of financing is much needed by developing countries during a commodity crisis such as the present one; yet the amounts available have proven inadequate: indeed, requests under the EEC's STABEX scheme, which was to perform a role similar to that of the CFF, have exhausted the resources of STABEX.

The Fund's CFF does not come close to compensating developing countries fully for temporary external shocks affecting the balance of payments. According to IMF data it has met less than one twelfth of African countries' terms of trade deterioration in the years 1978-81.[16] *We propose reforming the present quota-related restrictions on drawings under the CFF, and changing the coverage of the scheme and the methods by which shortfalls are calculated, and call for such changes to be made as a matter of urgency.*

Conditionality

This document proposes a major increase in the resources of the World Bank and the IMF. While that is desirable by itself, both the immediate and the somewhat longer-term purposes we have in mind would not be fully served without a change in lending policies of both institutions.

There is a connection between the magnitude of resources and the Fund's conditionality. Large quotas would permit countries to borrow more in the lower tranches. One of the biggest causes of resentment of IMF conditions in some countries is the sense of being forced to undergo painful policy changes for the sake of IMF loans which are very modest in amount. An IMF programme may be valuable not only because of the amount it lends, but also because its 'seal of approval' brings additional lending from other sources, especially for countries heavily involved in commercial rather than concessional borrowing. Studies suggest, however, that quite commonly the difficult adjustments poorer countries go through to obtain Fund credits have not been followed by substantial additional inflows of capital.[17]

Many countries today regard the IMF with mistrust, even hostility. There is something of a vicious circle here: because countries do not go to the IMF until they are *in extremis*, the measures the Fund then proposes are inevitably drastic, and its ogrish reputation is extended. And it is to some extent inevitable that the Fund incurs unpopularity. Countries often get into difficulty because they postpone politically awkward decisions. When their resulting loss of international creditworthiness finally forces them to seek the Fund's help, it is not surprising that the medicine prescribed is unpleasant.

In most cases, though, countries' problems arise from a mixture of domestic and external causes and, especially recently, the external factors have often been the most important. The question is, how can the relations between the Fund and its developing country members be improved so that – most particularly in the current acute stage of the world's financial disarray – it can play a much more positive part? One requirement would be for countries to approach the Fund 'at the onset of their problems', as our Report suggested. But that too would have to mean that countries could expect more substantial resources and more understanding conditions.

As already indicated, we fully accept that the revolving character of the Fund's resources has to be maintained; that it makes loans which will be repaid, and does not serve as an 'aid institution' (except insofar as lending is subsidised for low-income borrowers, as it already is); that countries' balance of payments deficits must be seen to be moving to elimination in the requisite period; and that to the extent that unsatisfactory policies have been contributing factors in a country's being in deficit, these must be corrected. But within these constraints there is scope for giving greater weight to other objectives – not just adjustment to balance of payments deficits and the control of inflation, but growth, employment and the equitable distribution of incomes. There is typically more than one way of achieving external equilibrium; but the Fund generally assumes a very limited range of possibilities. The Fund should also have a counter-cyclical role, not, as has often been the case since mid-1981, that of reinforcing avoidable contraction: in particular it should avoid advocating policies for a number of countries which, when carried out by all of them together, will reduce world income and employment at a time when expansion is needed.

Our Report referred to a number of criticisms of the Fund's conditionality: that it concentrated excessively on a monetary approach to balance of payments analysis, that it did not give countries adequate time to adjust, that political realities were insufficiently considered. Recent studies[18] have reinforced these concerns and pointed to others. The Fund's concentration on demand control, devaluation and credit ceilings as the main instruments of policy minimises the importance of other measures: those on the supply side for example, not least where the supply of goods for export is in question.

The Fund often looks primarily to *price* incentives, whereas price responses may be slow and initially weak, especially in less advanced countries. It insists on conditions of liberalised imports, often excessively. Our next chapter expresses a strong commitment to an open trading environment. But the GATT recognises the special problems of developing countries. And even the industrial countries need their temporary 'safeguards'. Less advanced countries are still more vulnerable to disruptive imports. The Fund *must* respect far more than it does each country's capacity to transform its economy, which depends considerably on its stage of development. 'Uniformity of treatment' means like treatment for like cases, not identical treatment for all cases.

Sometimes the public expenditure cuts in Fund programmes damage the capacity to effect needed changes in economic structure and productivity improvement. Some credit restrictions may actually worsen the balance of payments if, for example, they limit industrial capacity utilisation by curbing inventories or working capital. Fund programmes might look quite different if the balance between supply- and demand-oriented measures was altered in the direction of the former, and the maximum efforts were made to secure adjustment with growth, or at least to minimise the economic and social costs of demand restriction, should that be unavoidable. The importance of the relationship between World Bank Structural Adjustment Loans (SAL) and Fund EFF credits, and thus between Bank and Fund conditionality, is obvious in this context. In fact, a country is usually expected by the Bank to reach agreement with the Fund first on a standby or EFF credit when it initially applies for a SAL. This is an unfortunate sequence, effectively relegating supply-side adjustment issues to a secondary place in policy formulation, given the Fund's current approach to conditionality.

Pace of adjustment
It is undoubtedly over demand management and devaluation that the greatest problems have arisen between the Fund and members seeking standbys. When countries have permitted excessive expansion and allowed the exchange rate to become over-valued rather than take corrective action, tighter fiscal and credit policies and devaluation eventually become necessary. What matters to

the countries are the pace and extent of change. The Fund has even in recent times advocated shock treatment for countries where it has only a slender chance of being effective. It should recognise more fully that, especially in poorer and less adaptable countries, if unsatisfactory policies have been in operation over a period of years they cannot often be 'put right' by sudden about-faces, drastic devaluations overnight and the like. Where difficulties are principally due to a harsh external environment, such an approach is even more misplaced. Again, the situation of the less advanced countries must be more adequately reflected in their treatment. Proposals for devaluation often fail to take adequately into account that the resulting lower export prices may not generate larger sales. Commodity exporters will not benefit from devaluation when commodity markets are crumbling – or if they do, only at other exporters' expense.

Even for countries which are in a position to respond to stern measures, it is pointless to press corrective action to the point where political upheaval will result, as happened in Egypt, for example, or Sudan, in recent years. This may mean on occasion tolerating a more gradual reduction of inflation than the Fund might ideally like: in many developing countries unemployment is so serious and so volatile an issue that it has to be given greater weight in policy formulation.

It should not be suggested that negotiations with the Fund are always difficult and its programmes always harsh. On the contrary, many countries have had perfectly satisfactory negotiations with the Fund and benefited from the programmes, as our Report observed. If the Fund can acquire a record for greater understanding, consistently – as we insist is feasible – with its mandate, its role can only become more productive.

At least it would avoid having a counter-productive reputation – of a kind which made Brazil, for example, implement an austerity programme in 1981 and 1982 without Fund assistance. The programme was much like one the Fund would have proposed, but Brazil did not have the benefit of Fund resources, and its government could not ask for them for fear of ensuing unpopularity – surely an absurd state of affairs for all concerned. The lessons of this and many other cases must be learned. The premier institution for adjustment cannot remain a place to be shunned by those who need it most.

Monitoring Fund programmes
Some of the difficulties countries have with the Fund relate to the criteria embodied in the agreement on a credit, especially the quantitative criteria. These are often specified in an inflexible manner, and can lead to curtailment of a programme if the Fund deems that essential conditions have been violated. The studies of the Fund referred to above have suggested reforms – for example, that assumptions on which programmes are based could be set out fully: assumptions about inflation rates, interest rates, the terms of trade, output of crops, and so on. If the assumptions prove wrong, countries (and the Fund as well) should have the right to seek a revision in the performance criteria (and perhaps also in the scale of their drawings). One study also suggests making targets more flexible for important aspects of the economy, and distinguishing between ceilings and targets. 'Some of the ill-will with which negotiations with the Fund are regarded might be eased if it were agreed that the projections would provide targets and that the sanctions associated with performance criteria would come into play only if the targets were exceeded by such a wide margin as to breach a ceiling set a specified distance from the target.'[19]

Conditionality: proposals
To summarise, we propose on conditionality:

● That the IMF's conditionality be made more appropriate to the situation of the borrower, especially with respect to countries' capabilities to borrow in commercial markets, their needs for balance of payments support from official agencies, and their abilities to correct payments deficits over given time periods. In particular low-income countries with limited access to market borrowing, heavy dependence on official agencies for balance of payments support, and restricted capacity for rapid economic transformation, should have far greater availability of low conditionality finance when temporary deficits arise due to circumstances beyond their control.

- That countries be encouraged by the enlarged availability of low-conditionality credits to come to the IMF at an early stage of anticipated difficulties.
- That the IMF use its expanded resources to give countries support for expansionary adjustment wherever possible.
- That greater attention be paid to supply relative to demand conditions, so that payments deficits are corrected by an appropriate mix of policies with less exclusive concentration on demand constraints, devaluation and credit ceilings as the main instruments of adjustment.
- That the IMF in framing its programmes give greater weight to output, growth, employment and income-distribution considerations, relative to its past emphasis on the control of inflation and demand management, and that it obey more fully its own new guidelines of 1979 which call for paying 'due regard to the domestic, social and political objectives of member countries'.
- That the IMF observe particular sensitivity to members' stage of economic development when prescribing certain policy changes, such as those involved in import liberalisation, devaluation and the setting of domestic price incentives, bearing in mind that some countries will benefit much less quickly than others from such changes.
- That quantitative criteria embodied in Fund programmes be made more flexible, and in particular

(a) that the assumptions about the future course of important economic variables be spelt out in agreements with the Fund, so that if their actual course differed substantially from that assumed, performance criteria and the scale of drawings could be revised, and (b) that targets for performance be specified, with suitable margins of deviation such that sanctions associated with failing to meet performance criteria would be applied only if the target were missed by an agreed margin.

Terms and subsidies

The IMF has a subsidy account and also a Trust Fund (financed separately from other Fund facilities) with which it makes concessional loans to low-income countries. The Trust Fund's resources are now fully committed, and the subsidy account applies to past credits under the Supplementary Financing Facility, and not to the Enlarged Access Policy that has replaced it. Given the large number of low-income countries now forced to borrow from the Fund, the resources for subsidising loans need increasing. SDRs bear market rates of interest, and other Fund credits are only a few percentage points below market rates, so without further subsidies, the increase in Fund resources proposed here will not be on terms suitable for the low-income members. For the poorest countries, as our Report proposed, the timing of repayments should also be made more flexible, 'so that they are linked to the borrowers' capacity to repay'. In recent negotiations with Tanzania for example, projections suggested the country's exports needed to grow some 4–6 per cent faster to meet all its obligations including those incurred under a proposed Fund programme – but even that modest improvement might be very difficult for the country during the present recession.

There are a number of possible sources of subsidy funds. The largest single source in the past has been sales of IMF gold; we propose further, controlled, gold sales. Secondly, industrial countries could voluntarily transfer SDRs to the subsidy account. Thirdly repayments from the Trust Fund could be channelled to this account. Fourthly, contributions from members could be sought for this purpose, as has been done in the past. And fifthly, richer countries could be charged full market rates on funds which they presently borrow on concessional terms, the savings thus obtained going to the subsidy account. We propose that some combination of these measures be used to enlarge the subsidy account, particularly for the benefit of the poorest countries.

The World Bank and International Development Association

We have given so much space to the IMF because it is the principal international institution capable of acting swiftly in the present situation. The World Bank has traditionally concerned itself with longer-term development, mainly through project lending. This separation of functions is right and proper. Some of the new problems of the world economy have, however, brought about an unavoidable overlap between the desirable functions of the Fund and the Bank, especially in the area of structural adjustment. But if the Bank's contributions to development have hitherto looked to a more distant horizon, they are nonetheless important and urgent.

We first of all make a strong plea for a re-dedication of all the industrial countries to support the International Development Association, or IDA, the World Bank's concessional lending arm. Low-income countries receive assistance on terms they can afford mainly from IDA, the United Nations agencies and bilateral donors. All these sources of assistance are valuable. But there are special reasons for wishing to ensure the continued strength of IDA. Because of its size the World Bank group has become the main focus for development policy discussions between aid giver and recipient; it also helps to coordinate aid policy among all donors for a number of countries through aid consortia and consultative groups. Because it is relatively free from the foreign policy and commercial pressures which surround national, bilateral aid programmes, IDA can give primacy to development criteria in aid allocation, in terms both of the nature of its projects and of the countries to which it lends – 81 per cent of its lending goes to low-income countries, and a further 17 per cent to countries with *per capita* incomes just above the 'low-income' boundary.

IDA receives its funds from industrial and OPEC member governments, and some other developing countries, in three-year 'replenishments'. It was the US decision to spread over four years its agreed commitment to the sixth IDA replenishment ('IDA VI') that led to the drop in IDA lending in 1981-82 to $2.7 billion; this will now rise to $3.3 billion in the current financial year and $3.7 billion in 1983-84, thanks to the agreement reached in Toronto. But that agreement was a stop-gap measure and IDA's future is not assured. *It is imperative that there be a generous response by all donors in the negotiations for IDA VII, leading to a substantial increase of IDA funding in real terms.*

In this context the question of 'graduation' in IDA also arises. A US Treasury study[20] gave as a reason (the only reason, apart from 'shortage of budgetary funds') for withdrawing support from IDA, that some countries could be 'graduated' out of IDA, that is, treated as middle-income countries, not requiring concessional assistance. The only major borrowers whose 'graduation' would make a significant difference are India and China. They may be managing relatively well in the present crisis. But they too can suffer from climatic and other natural disasters which can set back the entire economy. They contain more poor *people* than the combined populations of all the least developed countries, and their resources to combat their problems are severely limited, and cannot be supplemented on a longer-term basis by large borrowing on market terms. They have more developed human resources and larger industrial sectors than the least developed countries; but they are by all other criteria among the poorest countries. As a World Bank study has said, 'Maintaining the proper balance between the competing claims of India, China and sub-Saharan Africa will be a major issue during the next decade.'[21] Balance, yes; 'graduation', no. A larger IDA is needed to accommodate additional demands on it; it should neither be reduced to remove current major borrowers, nor have its terms hardened.

Programme lending
We believe more funds should be available for the Bank's programme of Structural Adjustment Loans (SAL). These are presently limited by the Bank's rule that not more than 10 per cent of Bank group lending should be in programme (or non-project) form. We argued in the Report that this rule was ripe for change. The case is, if anything, even stronger now that the need for structural adjustment is so widespread. This policy change is needed not only because of the SAL programme, but also to permit the Bank more scope in other forms of programme lending. The Bank as well as the Fund has a role to play in balance of payments support, and its sector and other programme loans and its finance for local cost expenditure could and should make a greater contribution. As noted above, and as argued in our Report, project lending alone – however important – has clear limitations in promoting development, especially in low-income countries.

In the current circumstances of acute balance of payments pressure, poor countries find it even harder than usual to find the matching domestic and foreign-exchange resources for new investment projects. Today the Bank is having to make considerable supplemental loans to enable countries to continue projects which have already started; for the same reasons, in many countries it is extremely difficult to launch further projects of a traditional kind at all. Programmes of agricultural development, education and other poverty-oriented investment on the required scale cannot succeed if international assistance is confined largely to the capital costs of projects. Further, research in the last decade – not least that of the World Bank itself – has demonstrated that schooling, health services, nutritional programmes and other provision of 'basic needs' have a high economic return as well as being essential to elementary human welfare.[22] For the poorest countries, development cannot take place without them.

Paying teachers' or health workers' salaries *is* investment, investment in human resources: such costs should be regarded as just as worthy of aid support as building factories or supplying machinery and equipment. The Bank group (and many other donors) already accept this case and support local and recurrent costs and programme loans. But these purposes could absorb substantially greater resources, particularly in the poorest countries. Even in more expansive times the 10-per-cent rule is unduly restrictive: in times such as the present it prevents the Bank from pursuing its own objectives and meeting its borrowers' critical needs. *We therefore propose that the Bank group's programme lending for balance of payments support and sectoral development be permitted to rise to 30 per cent of commitments in any one year.*

The World Bank's resources

The above proposals refer to measures required for immediate Bank and IDA operations. We must also address the question of augmenting the World Bank's borrowing authority. The Bank raises most of its funds by borrowing, issuing World Bank bonds. It does so on the basis of its guaranteed capital – callable or paid-in – subscribed by member governments. But its capital/borrowing ratio is extremely conservative, one-to-one. Our Report proposed that it be raised to one-to-two, which would still leave it very conservative by comparison with commercial banks' one-to-twenty or more.

The Bank was being advised by some financial experts in

1982 that, given the shakiness of financial markets, the solidity of the Bank's financing should not be disturbed by a change in the gearing ratio. Another objection has been that existing World Bank bonds have been issued on the basis of one-to-one capital backing, and would be affected by a change in the gearing ratio. Neither of these objections is insuperable. Many bankers would not agree with the first and would welcome a larger role for the Bank created by such means; and the second is a legal technicality which can be overcome.

Thus we believe the proposal was and is sound. The Bank will need to raise more funds in the near future both for its own activities and – as we suggest below – to collaborate further with private lending. *We propose* therefore *that discussion of doubling the Bank's gearing ratio proceed so that the measure can be adopted as soon as practicable.* If necessary the ratio could be raised on a step-by-step basis, some percentage points at a time, so that the new ratio is approached over a period of a very few years. The alternative method of increasing the Bank's borrowing capacity is by capital increases (subscribed even if not paid-in capital); *either a change in the gearing ratio or a new capital increase is essential, or a combination of both.*

Another approach would be initially to set up a segregated capital account to which new capital would be subscribed. This capital would be used on a higher gearing ratio, say one-to-two or even more for new bond issues, leaving existing Bank bonds and capital unaffected. Such a new account could be used for a variety of purposes, including the new energy agency proposed in Chapter 4, if it were set up as an affiliate of the Bank. Such a segregated capital account we would see as a step towards the proposal in our Report for changing the gearing ratio of the Bank's borrowing generally, to which we adhere – not as an alternative to it. The proposal would also test market reactions to this proposed new basis of Bank borrowing: it is not obvious that the market acceptability of bonds raised in this way would differ significantly from existing Bank bonds.

World Bank conditionality
We stress the role of multilateral agencies in part because of their capacity to influence policy. However, we have a serious reservation. The power to influence policies will be entrenched by increased resources. That power must be sensitively employed. We devoted a good deal of space to Fund conditionality. But frictions have also arisen in the past between the World Bank and its clients. The Bank itself is finding that the conditions of some of its Structural Adjustment Loans have been excessive and countries have not been able to carry them out. The Bank's recent Africa study[23] aroused interest with its diagnosis of the problems; but its prescriptions, which seemed to put excessive faith in the possibilities of rapid change through more widely used market incentives, were much criticised. Coming out at a time when some of the World Bank's industrial country members seemed to be putting pressure on the Bank for more emphasis on private enterprise, it naturally gave rise to concern.

We would agree that countries – especially those which lack the trained personnel to make bureaucracies efficient – could often give much greater weight to the appropriateness of price and fiscal incentives to enhance productive efficiency. But the Bank's Articles enjoin it to respect its members' different economic systems, as indeed it does in most of its operations. There is a strong current mood in the donor community to require greater efforts by aid recipients to improve their own economic performance. If this secures more support for aid in the donor countries and genuine improvements in policies by the recipients, it can only be welcomed. But the 'dialogue' on policies between agencies and borrowing countries must be a dialogue, not an imposition of alien views; and the fundamental objectives and constraints of the recipients' social, political and economic values and strategies must be respected. Finally let it not be forgotten – as the Africa study emphasised – that policy reform is not a substitute for more assistance; it *requires* more assistance to be successful.

Aid
Multilateral aid comprises just over one quarter of aid, or Official Development Assistance (ODA). IDA represents slightly less than one eighth of all aid. The rest of ODA consists of bilateral programmes. We are concerned with the total of ODA and its quality. In 1981 aid reached a total of $35.5 billion. While aid has risen substantially over the past twenty years, it has fallen as a proportion of the donors' GNP: it was half of one per cent of their GNP in the early 1960s; since the 1970s it has fluctuated around 0.35 per cent, half the target of 0.7 per cent to which most donors committed themselves more than a decade ago.

Some countries contribute more than that target. OPEC countries' aid, one fifth of all ODA today, was equivalent to 1.46 per cent of their GNP in 1981, and was substantially higher than that in the capital-surplus OPEC countries. The Netherlands and the Scandinavian countries also exceeded the target. Towards the other end of the scale lie the UK (0.44 per cent), Canada (0.43), Australia (0.41), Japan (0.28), the United States (0.20) and Italy (0.19).[24] For the immediate future, while several donors have indicated increases in aid, some – most notably the US – look like reducing theirs below previously expected levels. In our Report we observed that if GNP were growing at the rates of the 1970s, the allocation of a tiny fraction of the annual increment to GNP would close the gap between existing levels and the 0.7-per-cent target in only five years. We called for this gap to be closed in four years by 1985. Given that GNP has grown very little, it would perhaps have been too much to expect substantial progress towards that goal. But in 1981, aid in real value and as a share of DAC members' GNP actually fell – for that there is no excuse. *We urge the donors to set their*

74

sights once more on the fulfilment of the 0.7-per-cent target, and reach it in five years. Bilateral aid donors must also give a higher proportion of their aid in the form of programme lending.

The poorest countries

In the meantime there are subsidiary ambitions which could be fulfilled with less strain on the donors' budgets. The highest priority must be for increased aid to the poorest countries. One of the most important proposals of the Commission's Report was for increased and improved financial aid to the poverty belts of Africa and Asia. Aid to the United Nations' list of least developed countries in fact increased fairly fast after the mid-1970s. Bilateral aid to these countries from members of the OECD's Development Assistance Committee (DAC) grew at 8.4 per cent a year in real terms between 1974-80, compared with 3–4 per cent for total Official Development Assistance; it constitutes 19.6 per cent of their bilateral aid. For OPEC countries it has also risen, but still constitutes only 14.9 per cent of their bilateral aid. Multilateral agencies increased the volume of aid going to the least developed countries even faster, by 19.4 per cent annually between 1974-80. Total net aid disbursements to these countries reached $6.1 billion in 1980 (though they fell to $5.5 billion in 1981).

Nevertheless, there are very considerable unmet needs in the poverty belts; aid to them did not increase commensurately with the increased need in the crisis period since 1979, nor commensurately with the scale proposed in our Emergency Programme. Nor are there yet agreed 'long-term plans to set these regions on the path of lasting growth' as the Report proposed.

A UN Conference on Least Developed Countries, held in Paris in September 1981, concluded with a commitment by 'most' donor countries to reach a target of 0.15 per cent of GNP for the least developed countries (within the overall 0.7-per-cent target); others would 'double' their aid to these countries, so that overall, by 1985, they should receive twice the aid they had in the five years up to 1981. But the commitment was vague, with no specification of whether constant or current values were agreed and with some donor countries not willing to commit themselves to precise targets. Some agreement was reached on improvements in aid practices and management. The Conference also addressed a number of other issues including trade, and the improvement of domestic economic management. These other measures are important: more aid by itself is not enough. But even the target of a doubling of aid in real terms would be less than is needed to make a major and durable change in the poorest countries' prospects. The figures sound large in billions of dollars. But divided up among thirty-five developing countries – one of which, Bangladesh, has a population of over ninety million – the amounts are not overwhelming.

A recent World Bank simulation for Africa showed the effects of combined aid increases and policy improvements. 'With continuation of present policies and only a small increase in aid . . . *per capita* GDP is projected to fall throughout the 1980s . . . With appropriate policy reforms the prospects brighten . . . Policy reform without substantially increased aid, however, does not provide a satisfactory solution . . . *Moreover, many African countries could not undertake reform without additional assistance.* [A near doubling of aid in real terms] combined with policy reforms could increase *per capita* incomes in oil-importing Africa by nearly one quarter during the coming decade compared with virtual stagnation without it.'[25]

We urge the donors to double by 1985, in real terms, the aid flows which the poorest countries received in the five years up to 1981, and to reach and maintain a target for such aid of 0.15 per cent of GNP. A substantial IDA VII would of course contribute significantly to that goal. *We also urge the donors to fulfil earlier undertakings on official debt, that all such debt be waived in respect of all the least developed countries.*

The UN agencies and Regional Development Banks
Another set of aid channels presently starved of funds are the United Nations agencies. In a recent report the Director General for Economic Development observed that projected resources were only three quarters of what had been expected. The UK and US had cut their contributions by 10 per cent. The United Nations Development Programme was particularly hard hit. We believe this parsimony to be ill-considered, even if there is room for improvement in some of the programmes in question, and *we urge the donor community to restore the funding of these agencies on an adequate basis.* Our Report also made a number of proposals for enlarging and strengthening the Regional Development Banks – these too must not be allowed to languish.

Country allocation of aid
One way to secure more aid for low-income countries even within existing aid totals would be to change the country distribution of aid. At present about 40 per cent of all aid goes to middle-income countries – nearly all of it bilateral aid; as noted, the multilateral agencies devote the bulk of their concessional funds to the low-income countries. Of course much of this is due to political and military-strategic considerations. It is hard to divert such aid to countries whose needs for aid on developmental criteria are much greater: but efforts should be made. There is of course a wide variety of countries in the 'middle-income' group. Some have become aid donors themselves; others are only just above the dividing line between low-income and middle-income and – especially in the current situation – require concessional assistance. But there must be a presumption that some aid at least could be switched from better-off to poorer countries.

We particularly deplore a practice seen with increasing

frequency in recent times, namely the offer of Official Development Assistance to quite well-off developing countries to help the donor secure profitable export orders, aid which would otherwise go to poorer countries. This offends the spirit of the GATT and the Berne Union agreement on credit competition. There is a case for excluding from definitions of aid all concessional assistance extended to countries above a certain level of *per capita* income; such aid should not count towards the fulfilment of aid targets.

Aid effectiveness: the impact on poverty
Many critics of aid believe, on the basis of a few glaring examples of misused or unsuccessful aid loans – often belonging to the distant past – that aid is not effectively used. In fact the great bulk of it is effective. IDA projects, for example, have a weighted average rate of return of 21 per cent, excellent by any standards.[26] We believe all donor governments would agree with our statement in the Report that 'the overwhelming proportion of aid money is usefully spent on the purposes for which it is intended'. A criticism more common nowadays is that high rates of return do not necessarily imply a powerful impact on poverty. It certainly is true that until a few years ago donors were concerned less with the impact on poverty than with the impact on growth or overall development.

This by no means implies that aid not directly aimed at alleviating poverty has had no impact on the poor; on the contrary. It would be simplistic to assume either that all aid should be designed for a direct impact on poverty, or that any which is not is undesirable. Much of the past aid which has gone into infrastructure or industrial schemes may not have done much directly for the poor; but it has helped to remove the constraints on development, development which alone can win the struggle against poverty.

Sharpening the focus of aid
The increasing consciousness in recent years that a larger

proportion of aid can and should be focused directly on the mitigation of poverty is much to be welcomed, provided it remains understood that other dimensions of development – including infrastructure and industry – must continue to receive attention. Poor countries must lay the foundations of growth in all the important sectors; they must be able to sustain public services, not become premature welfare states. But where – as in many of the poorest countries – the failure of rural development and the lack of educated and skilled people are major obstacles to growth, the alleviation of poverty and the promotion of some, at least, of traditional growth objectives point in similar directions.

Population and aid for the poorest
Indeed one can go further: one thing which has not changed in the last three years is the relation between development and population: that unless broadly based development reaches and changes the lives of ordinary people, rapid population growth will continue. Only as education spreads, as health programmes keep existing children alive, as families have secure incomes which do not depend on increasing their numbers, will incentives for large families disappear and population growth be kept within manageable bounds. Yet it is precisely such development which is threatened in the current crisis.

In some of the poorest countries populations are still growing at rates above 3 per cent a year, or doubling in less than twenty-five years. It is difficult for individual well-being to advance in such conditions; so much effort is required just to keep rapidly growing numbers from becoming worse off. Unless international assistance supports countries' efforts to extend programmes of human resource development and income generation for the poor, decline in population growth will not begin. Nor will it be possible to make real progress in the broader aims of development. *We urge aid donors and recipients to intensify their efforts to ensure that aid makes a greater contribution to the relief of poverty.*

Aid effectiveness and aid coordination

A particular need, especially in aid to the poorest countries, is for greater coordination among the donors. There was some media publicity in 1982 for the case of Upper Volta, whose officials had to field 360 visits of aid missions in a single year. The conclusion of large numbers of separate aid agreements each with its own terms and conditions and monitoring arrangements and other matters in fine print puts a tremendous strain on countries with limited administrative capacity.

Each donor's rules and regulations are designed in part to ensure accountability, in part so that the results are identifiable and the donor can receive credit for them. But this is unfortunate if it ends up accounting for inefficiency, and the identifiable results are less than optimal. Aid for the poorest countries needs channels of coordination, both for donors and recipients. Some exist already, but more integration is possible and desirable. Our Report made some suggestions, but we were far from being alone in stressing them. The OECD Development Assistance Committee has been engaged in a four-year study of aid coordination and effectiveness – we look to its findings being followed up.[27]

Voluntary agencies

In many of the aims of poverty-focused aid, private voluntary organisations of developed and developing countries such as religious organisations, trade unions, CARE, the International Red Cross, Médecins sans frontières, Oxfam, Save the Children, and numerous others have amassed valuable and successful experience. In meeting the needs of the poor at local level, in encouraging self-help and participation, in appreciating the social and cultural sensibilities of all the people involved, in circumventing bureaucratic red-tape and getting things done, they have a truly remarkable record.

They already collaborate in field activities with a variety of UN and other international agencies. Many of them have networks of volunteer or paid workers all over the Third World. They also have dedicated staffs in their home countries who collect the funds that pay for their activities, lobby and spread information for a variety of development causes, and play a major part in development education

We admire this activity and the people who engage in it. And we think it could receive more official support. In many countries governments already have schemes to match voluntary contributions with official ones. Given the effectiveness of these 'NGOs', or non-governmental organisations, especially in the very purpose of reducing poverty, we would like to see larger official subventions. They must be on a matching basis – anything else would change the nature of the organisations and their healthy dependence on voluntary contributions. But they could be more regular.

One method would be to adopt a common target, that all Northern governments should match on an agreed basis the privately contributed funds of voluntary agencies of recognised effectiveness. Another method, suggested to us by the director of one of the most successful voluntary agencies, would be to establish a new international facility, on its own or as part of an existing agency (such as UNICEF), with an annual fund of, say, $100 million which would be allocated to the private bodies on a matching basis with their own funds. Such a facility could also help to channel the knowledge of Third World needs possessed by these bodies to aid agencies and research institutions. Another possibility would be for donors to agree on an amount of such a magnitude, and distribute it through multilateral agencies, most of which already have NGO Liaison Units. These ideas appeal to us, and deserve further consideration.

Private capital flows
A large share of nineteenth- and early-twentieth-century

development of what is now the Third World was financed by risk capital, or equity – individuals and firms risking their money – without prospects of rescheduling – making fortunes or losing them. In some sense the commercial banks have assumed this role in recent years and it does not suit them as well, especially now that the volumes of capital are so large and the consequences of risk so fraught with danger. The risks are fairly well spread, and the consequences of interlinkage possibly exaggerated; but there were no threats to the financial system when the risks were shared by thousands upon thousands of companies and investors, a large number of whose loans or equity could become 'non-performing' without the risk spreading to others. From a purely financial point of view, it would be desirable for equity to play a much larger part in development finance today. Such an evolution would also accord with the perspectives of some of today's Northern governments, who would like to see more North–South cooperation take the form of private sector activities.

We believe that private business can play and has played an extremely valuable part in development and said as much in the Report. But our discussions made us aware of the complexities of the relationship between the private sector and development, and of what was necessary to improve that relationship. Much has already been said about private flows through the banking system. But what about private investment?

Overseas investment
Private foreign investment is not exactly leaping ahead in developing countries. The unease with which private investors, especially multinational corporations, and the host countries look on each other has diminished greatly in recent years. And more and more technical cooperation has become available, through the United Nations, the Commonwealth Secretariat, and other organisations, to assist negotiations among the parties. Nevertheless, mutual suspicion remains. Many investors still worry about

operating conditions, taxation, repatriation of profits, renegotiation of contracts, perhaps above all political risk. And some host countries continue to fear exploitation, unfair contracts, concealment of information, transfer pricing, international cartelisation, restrictive business practices, distortion of pay or consumption patterns, and even political interference.

For all these and other reasons negotiations have been going on for many years, to establish codes of conduct and other procedures that would engender better relations between private foreign capital and developing countries. The measures proposed in Chapter 12 of our Report are highly desirable for long-term stability in the relationship between foreign investors and host countries; *we call for renewed efforts to negotiate a framework for international investment* such as we described there.

In the meantime there are other measures which could more rapidly assist the flow of private capital. Firstly, through *increased support for the IFC*, or International Finance Corporation, the World Bank group's facility for encouraging private investment. The IFC has recently completed a capital increase which permits it to expand its borrowing to support private investment; but for it to raise its risk-capital participation in private ventures in developing countries, which many would consider the most desirable path of expansion, more capital is needed and we urge that it be provided. Secondly, by multilateral investment insurance. A proposal for a Multilateral Investment Insurance Agency is currently being examined by the World Bank – *establishment of a mechanism along these lines should be pursued.*

As a source of finance to resolve immediate national payments problems, private investment can only play a small part. And we would emphasise that there is a large range of activities in which private capital cannot conceivably substitute for government-to-government lending. Nevertheless, we believe that strong efforts should be made to increase these flows and to ensure that their conditions are satisfactory both to investors and to the host countries.

Other private flows

There are also methods to increase the flow of private bank capital besides the institutional support discussed above. One would be through an increase in World Bank co-financing. Some have claimed that this does not provide much *additional* flow of private capital. In the last financial year only $3.25 billion of private bank capital was lent under the World Bank's scheme; it is argued that much of this would have been lent anyway; and some of the banks complained of the IBRD's lengthy procedures. These objections are not convincing. Co-financing does provide a useful channel for lending, especially for smaller banks which may be nervous of investing in the Third World in current circumstances. *We* therefore *support increases in the capital of the World Bank and Regional Development Banks to permit expanded co-financing.*

An interesting proposal is that for an Investment Credit Guarantee Fund, originally suggested by Mr H. J. Witteveen,[28] which would provide insurance for project lending by banks. The Fund would insure commercially viable projects (which satisfy absorptive capacity tests), with a minimum size of $10 million, against both project risks and country risks. The Fund is envisaged with shareholders' equity of $1 billion, of which only 10 per cent or $100 million need be paid up in cash; each share would be $10 million (of which $1 million in cash). An interest subsidy would be needed to assist participation of poorer countries. We believe this proposal merits further consideration by the international community.

Capital markets and current dangers

We have discussed a variety of measures to promote official and private capital flows. But our account would be incomplete without an examination of important features of the functioning of commercial capital markets, whose fragility has been the focus of a good deal of public and official attention in recent times.

One of the greatest fears has been the possibility of collapse in the banking system. 'Collapse' for a bank occurs when it cannot meet its financial obligations. Depositors anxious that this may happen attempt to withdraw their deposits, which can precipitate the collapse. Banks make provision for bad debts. But the amounts set aside for 'non-performing' loans reduce the banks' capital if the loans do not 'perform', that is, if interest is not paid on schedule; and reductions in capital reduce lending by a multiple, because banks are required to maintain a given ratio of capital to assets. (Loans, in bank accounting, are assets; deposits are liabilities.) If a large volume of its loans become non-performing a bank can be in serious trouble.

The biggest dangers of collapse related to Third World debt arise from the possibility of default by a major borrower. Usually a country will avoid default, since it may be regarded as unreliable for many years, even decades after the event and be unable to borrow from any source. It will prefer to reschedule or refinance its debt, seeking help from banks and international institutions. That of course implies that the latter can help, and in a manner acceptable to the borrowing country. But a country might just decide that its sufferings would be less if it simply refused to repay its debt rather than reduce domestic expenditures to meet foreign obligations. At present, it must be said, the biggest borrowers show no sign of taking such a view.

A country could be forced to default if it could not borrow enough to meet its obligations. In today's circumstances, the most important way that could happen with any real likelihood would be if banks withdrew from lending to a country in difficulties: they have no incentive to do this, as a group. But the smaller banks might try to 'get off the bus' and thus precipitate a crisis by not agreeing to reschedule or by declaring a borrower in default (a default to which other banks could be tied by cross-default clauses). If the country defaulted on its debts, a bank with assets in the country equivalent to a large share of that bank's total capital would indeed collapse. The probability that this will happen may be quite small. But the fear that it might can itself undermine confidence. A large number of reschedulings, cumulatively large in volume, could also have a strong adverse effect on banks' balance sheets, depending partly on the way bank regulators regard rescheduled debt.

Chain collapse?
The prospect of a 'chain collapse' in the financial system goes beyond the failure of a single bank, to envisage the possibility that several banks would collapse, either because other banks were directly affected by the failure of the first, or because a wave of loss of confidence on the part of depositors led to widespread withdrawals. (There were signs of weakening depositor confidence in the summer of 1982, but they had diminished by the end of the year.)

Today's interbank market is said by some to possess the potential of such 'knock-on' effects, for transmitting a collapse of one bank to others. Many analysts deny this; as long as each banking institution is soundly based the danger of 'chain collapse' is remote. Central banks will not permit a major bank to fold up. There are individual banks with uncomfortable looking asset-portfolios, and individual countries (which have borrowed from them) in dire economic straits. These are present dangers. We would emphasise the need for more systematic analysis of creditworthiness in lending to developing countries – analysis which takes as much account of the quality of economic management as of traditional economic indicators such as debt-service ratios, reserves and the like.

Bank regulation
Banks are of course not free to act as they please. Nationally they are subject to regulation – legal

regulation – by the count   . bank or other agency.
In turn the central ban'   lender of last resort to its
country's banks. If a crisis occurred and depositors lost
confidence and began withdrawing their deposits, the
central bank could lend to the bank in trouble and cover its
needs. The knowledge that this is so has in recent decades
prevented such crises of confidence: because they are
there, lender-of-last-resort facilities are rarely used. But it
is a weakness of the present world financial system that the
lender-of-last-resort function of central banks is not
clearly defined with respect to the overseas operations of
their national banks, and we would agree that this is a
matter deserving the closest attention on the part of
national authorities.

This is not to say that there is no regulation; on the
contrary, insofar as central banks' powers permit, they do
regulate aspects of their national banks' activities overseas.
The central banks' representatives meet in various fora,
and for these purposes, particularly in the Bank for
International Settlements (BIS) in Basle. Different
countries differ in the degree of supervision of lending by
their banks (or their banks' subsidiaries) overseas. Banks
and national authorities also have different attitudes to
doubtful-loan provisions and loan-risk assessment. This is
a subject of current concern, since it affects the way a
given bank's balance sheet will show losses and hence other
banks' assessments of it – and hence lending in the
'interbank market', the market in which banks borrow
from each other.

In recent times, in fact, national authorities have begun
to lay down stricter rules or guidelines on lending to
foreign countries and in particular the concentration of
country credit risk. This together with contraction in the
interbank market is now a further factor limiting the
expansion of Third World commercial borrowing.

An additional source of instability in the international
banking system is the lack of supervision in the operations
of the offshore capital market. Bank branches, or more

often their subsidiaries, which operate in the various offshore financial centres are not subject to the stringent regulation and control in respect of their reserves, liquidity ratios and gearing of capital to loan portfolio, such as exist *vis-à-vis* their internal currency deposits. The banks' profit-maximising objectives are restrained by their own individual banking prudence. Thus during the periods of the middle and late 1970s when the offshore markets were flush with funds, intense competition among lenders led to very fine spreads being offered to borrowers, causing some banks – particularly smaller ones – to cut into their reserves and reduce their liquidity ratios. Additionally, in the absence of clearly defined regulation in respect of liquidity provisions, the offshore banks while individually liquid may be *collectively* illiquid, particularly in the absence of lender-of-last-resort facilities for these offshore operations.

The Basle Agreement
Supervision does not except perhaps in rare cases extend to decisions about what specific loans a particular bank should make or not make. The supervisors are watching a *market*, and it is well understood by everyone that for most purposes the market must make its own choices, for good or ill, subject only to fundamental rules and prescriptions. The latter cannot guard absolutely against things going wrong, even badly wrong. The question is, who picks up the pieces if they do? The only statement of central banks' undertakings in this international field is in the famous and – deliberately – obscure 'Basle Agreement' of 1974. It says: 'it would not be practical to lay down in advance detailed rules and procedures for the provision of temporary liquidity', but that 'means are available for that purpose and will be used if and when necessary'.

In the current crisis many bankers and others have called for a clearer definition of central banks' responsibilities in the event of serious disruptions in the international capital market. Many others – not least bank supervisors themselves – resist such notions. The argument is that the clearer it is that help will come in time of trouble, and the more precisely the nature of that help is indicated, the less prudent banks will be tempted to be.

The argument is convincing. Besides, it is not conceivable that every eventuality could be forecast, with central banks' intended responses in each case precisely formulated. While improvements are needed in arrangements for debt rescheduling and supervision, the principal necessities in current circumstances are measures to expand net capital flows, commercial and official, and to ensure that the institution mainly responsible for assisting countries in balance of payments difficulties – the International Monetary Fund – be satisfactorily equipped to cope with emerging problems.

The response to the Mexican crisis of 1982 exhibited the strengths and weaknesses of existing arrangements. It was swift, and it included coordinated action by the IMF, the central banks (through the BIS) and the US government. But the IMF's programme is the core of the restructuring exercise, both the loan itself and the policies laid down. The central banks' finance, with the US providing additional supporting credits, was essentially a holding operation, until the Fund's programme could be agreed on and come into play. This episode showed that mechanisms exist, and how they could combine for a particular emergency. The need is to ensure their adequacy for the future.

A distinction should be kept between the IMF's role in relation to *countries* and the international financial system, supported as necessary by governments and central banks (it is this function to which the Basle Agreement refers); and individual central banks' responsibilities towards their national banks, which are a different matter. Longer-term strengthening of the international arrangements for handling international financial crises should be discussed within the context of a review of the Bretton Woods institutions such as we propose below.

Debt negotiations

With the increasing number and size of sovereign debt reschedulings there has been renewed questioning in many quarters about the process of commercial debt renegotiation. While it is still an *ad hoc* system, treating each case individually, a set of practices has been building up in the last two years. On the side of the banks a coordinating committee is established, representative by magnitude of exposure and by nationality, of all the banks involved. The government of the country too will receive advice, often from independent banking specialists from the private sector. Negotiations go on among all parties – the banks, the governments and the IMF, though cooperation between the Fund and the banks is not of a formal nature. The banks commonly like the Fund to be involved; it plays the major role in assessing the magnitude of the rescheduling required; the banks usually like the country to apply for Fund credits, the conditions for which help the banks to be assured of the country's future creditworthiness.

Other practices have also grown up. Banks consult among themselves through an Advisory Group in New York, originally set up in response to the Mexican case, and now continuing in a coordinating role. Numerous banks meet annually specifically to discuss the situation of individual major borrowing countries. As already noted, national bank supervisors and regulators increasingly keep a watchful eye on foreign lending, and coordinate their activities internationally. Nevertheless, there is still some cause for concern, and strengthening of the system is needed. Renegotiations are often lengthy and expensive. The treatment countries receive is variable; governments also complain that their responsibilities to their creditors are taken more seriously than their responsibilities to their citizens. More 'prevention' rather than 'cure' is deemed desirable by many observers.

Neither countries nor banks can be forced to the negotiating table; even if a country were advised to take early action, it need not heed the advice. The banks too may not wish to lend to countries even after the Fund's 'seal of approval' – or they may wish to lend even without it; they have to judge their own interests independently. But Fund programmes have become more and more the necessary condition for bank reschedulings. If our proposals on Fund conditionality were followed and the developing countries found the Fund less unsympathetic to their problems, relationships between all parties would be easier. Though it is essential that the changes in conditionality we propose be understood for what they are: more relevant, not less 'tough'. The banks have to be convinced that countries will make appropriate adjustments; otherwise the 'seal of approval' will not work.

Official debt
Mechanisms for dealing with official debt may be better established and less time-consuming than they are for commercial bank debt but many of the concerns are the same. Since 1956 official debt renegotiations have taken place on a multilateral basis at Paris Club meetings of the principal creditor countries, with the World Bank, IMF and, in recent years, UNCTAD attending as observers. As with commercial debt, creditors will not consider a request for rescheduling until after a debt problem has emerged. Also, since 1966 creditors have required the debtor to agree to a stabilisation programme with the IMF as a precondition of a Paris Club meeting. Having agreed to a rescheduling the Paris Club determines its amount (normally 80 per cent of principal repayments in arrears or falling due within a two-year period) and its duration (normally ten years). The interest rate is usually left to individual creditors to determine. In some instances, however, the terms have varied greatly from these norms.

Developing countries would like to submit their own plans for achieving resolution of debt problems, in a forum of their own choosing, with the World Bank and

IMF offering no more than analysis and advice, and to initiate action at an early stage when a country believes it faces difficulties involving debt. UNCTAD resolutions in 1978 and 1980 proposed such a system for official debt. Northern governments argue that the existing *ad hoc* arrangements have worked well on the whole and require only minor modification.

In line with our earlier proposals, however, we would wish to see the World Bank more closely involved, especially with the debt problems of poorer countries, and especially when longer-term, structural adjustment is called for. The Bank and Fund together could, at the debtor country's request, jointly convene meetings with other creditors to discuss debt rescheduling, and could together consult on steps to avoid future difficulties and on adjustment programmes. In these circumstances due regard could be given to social and political conditions, and some of the harshness of some past programmes be avoided. *We urge the strengthening of informal coordination among the IMF, the World Bank, other official lenders and the commercial banks in negotiations on debt rescheduling or to overcome severe financial difficulties, with a view to ensuring adequate provision of resources through the support of all lenders.*

Funding developing countries' debt
Further approaches to the debt problem are also important. There are a variety of proposals for funding developing countries' debt.[29] Essentially this implies devising a form of long-term borrowing by developing countries. Our proposals above would, we believe, hold the present critical situation and permit considerable improvement over the next year or two and beyond. But there is a good case for moving away from the large volumes of floating-rate debt contracted in recent years, and for transforming the maturity structure of debts. Unless that maturity structure is transformed, it will be difficult to do much more than try to anticipate debt crises

and prevent their doing too much damage. And if recent moves towards lower interest rates prove not to be a sustained trend, such funding may become a more urgent need: some commentators believe it is already urgent – certainly if it could be organised it would contribute greatly to relieving the present debt problem.

Long-term borrowing of this kind would require the issue of bonds, the proceeds of whose sale would go to developing countries. The bonds would need a sponsor or issuing agency, which could be an existing international institution, or a new agency. They would need guarantees, which could be provided in part by the agency and in part by developing countries themselves. They would need a procedure for currency denomination – the SDR being the obvious choice. Issuing and lending arrangements would obviously also require elaboration.

Such a proposal would not only alleviate the debt problem; it could also help to fill the gap identified in our Report as a missing element in development finance, that of long-term programme lending. And it could (though it need not) be linked to another proposal put forward for consideration in our Report, the creation of a new international financial institution, a World Development Fund (WDF). The need for further long-term programme lending to complement the World Bank's long-term project loans and the IMF's shorter-term adjustment finance is unlikely to be filled by existing institutions even if all the 'immediate' proposals above are implemented. Nor would these proposals lead to the changes in developed–developing country financial relations which the WDF was designed to bring about.

Rediscounting and consolidating debt
A related idea could also be considered, namely a 'rediscounting' of some part of developing countries' private bank debt. An agency would purchase developing countries' obligations to banks, but at a discount: that is, the banks would receive, say, $90–95 in exchange for $100

of the debt taken over by the agency. The 'agency' could be organised by governments or central banks of the industrial countries; perhaps the BIS could be such an agency. The developing countries' debts would be renegotiated, and having been taken over at a discount, could have their maturities stretched out and interest rates reduced without budgetary cost to the industrial countries.

The agency or its constituent institutions would be assuming the risk on these obligations, but acquiring them at a price reflecting that risk. Part of the cost would be paid by the participating banks, which would be accepting a loss on their loans. This might be attractive to them in some circumstances – perhaps particularly to smaller banks. At present banks have little choice but to keep the loans on their books, or write them off completely. Some form of mid-way option could be desirable.

An alternative would be for central banks or governments to assist interested banks in converting some short-term developing-country obligations into longer-term assets, leaving the process of renegotiating or rescheduling medium- and long-term debt unaltered. Under yet a third possibility, syndicated loans to different countries could be 'packaged' by an agency which took them over from banks – at a discount – and then combined debt of several countries into an instrument which could be marketed under the agency's full or partial guarantee.

Developing countries would have their debt alleviated directly only under the first scheme, which would provide for renegotiation of debt. The other two schemes would mainly benefit the banks. But since their balance-sheets could be improved under all the schemes, there could be more stability in capital markets, and stimulation of new lending.

However, there are many other considerations. The taking of such action might give market signals which are harmful to developing countries' borrowing prospects. Several banks and developing countries would not like it thought that their commercial paper was worth anything

94

less than 100 per cent of its face value. Perhaps banks would not wish to see measures of this kind adopted until it was obvious that continued rescheduling was not going to be possible by existing methods.

All the pros and cons of these ideas need to be weighed carefully. Still others have been proposed for national or international action.[30] Our concern is simply that they be aired for further consideration.

For the future: the Bretton Woods institutions

Our proposals on the IMF and World Bank above comprehend the necessary expansion and changes in policies essential to allow the Bank and IMF to function adequately in the current dangerous period. They do not reflect the recommendations for more pervasive reform of these institutions expressed in our Report, which we continue to advocate. Part of that reform was to bring about a greater measure of power sharing, widening the international basis of management and decision-making. Without that, the less adversarial relations between the Fund and its members which we would like to see will not be fully attained. Nor will the still large surpluses of some of the members from the South be readily put at the disposal of the Bretton Woods institutions.

We would like to see a more systematic and fully multilateral approach to countries in critical financial situations, rather than present *ad hoc* arrangements. This could include evolution of the IMF in the direction of carrying out some of the functions of an international central bank. For these and many other reasons we welcome the many voices now added to our own calling for a review of the Bretton Woods institutions. We believe this should be an authoritative, international review which should lead to an international conference on their reform. We stress that the agenda of reform should include attention to the question of power sharing which, as we point out in Chapter 5, also has important conseqences for other international negotiations.

We have already referred to the need for exchange-rate stabilisation. But we would also expect the wider objectives of international monetary reform to be taken up, including in our view the establishment of the SDR as the principal international reserve asset, the substitution account, and a defined role in global adjustment for surplus as well as deficit countries. These were proposed not only by our Report but by large numbers of experts who have examined the fundamental needs of the monetary system. They have been through ups and downs of international negotiations. Negotiations must be resumed, with a commitment to success.

In our Report we called for the extension of the IDA replenishment period from three to five years. In today's political climate this may be an idea whose moment has not yet come; but we still hold to its validity. Immediately, nothing should interfere with maintaining IDA at satisfactory levels in the near term. But it would be a demonstration of international commitment to the principles of multilateralism, which we strongly support, and to the cause of development of the poorer countries, to secure the continuing future of IDA on a longer-term basis. We would hope that the international community will in due course move in this direction. The same is true of the UN agencies, several of which are even worse off than IDA, being funded on a year-to-year basis. Their financing too must be put on a more secure footing.

A World Development Fund

The Report asked for international consideration of a particularly far-reaching proposal; it called for a 'move towards greater equality and partnership' between North and South in financial institutions; universal membership, including full representation of East European countries; new lending policies, especially long-term programme lending, export credits and commodity financing; and the channelling of new resources raised on an international basis. It suggested these could be the roles of a World

Development Fund. *We believe discussion of this new institution should have a secure place on the agenda of the Global Negotiations to be conducted in the United Nations.*

South–South financial cooperation
The Report recommended support for payments and clearing arrangements, credit agreements, 'reserve pools', export credit finance and refinancing arrangements among developing countries. Many of these have been features of sub-regional or regional integration schemes. There is not a great deal of progress to report. The following measures have scope for considerable progress:

● *Strengthening payments arrangements.* A dozen such arrangements have come into being recently at sub-regional or regional level. They could be strengthened and extended to promote regional and inter-regional trade. They could also be developed further into mutual balance of payments support arrangements for participating countries, if finance were forthcoming.
● *Expansion of developing countries' financial facilities.* Some developing countries have been extending bilateral assistance to others, and multilateral assistance has been provided, primarily by OPEC countries. These flows could be more effective if they incorporated a larger proportion of long-term programme lending. There has for some time been talk of the possibility that the OPEC Fund would become a fully-fledged development finance agency. Among many developing countries interest today centres on the possibility of establishing a Third-World Bank.
● *Increased developing country participation in regional development banks.* Existing plans to expand the capital base of these banks will offer productive and secure investment for capital surplus developing countries; such participation could help to make these banks' management and decision-making more

responsive to their clients' needs for programme lending and conditionality related to their development plans. Developing countries could show their commitment to these banks by placing part of their reserves on deposit with them, even if at some sacrifice of interest.

● *Export credit guarantee facilities.* Some institutions already offer export financing facilities to member developing countries; but many areas lack such mechanisms. There is a need for an institution of considerable scale which would buy or guarantee credit bills for national export credit agencies (which allow the exporter to be paid in local currency) so that they could be sold in international financial markets. The exporting country could then receive early payment of foreign exchange.

Our Report also spoke of a number of possibilities of direct investment by surplus developing countries, or triangular cooperation with their resources and technology from industrial or other developing countries. We urge developing countries to promote all these forms of cooperation and to support them with their own financial strength.

International revenues

We would not like the most 'futuristic' of all the Report's proposals to be lost completely from view, namely those for international 'automatic' revenue generation from a variety of possible sources, including levies on the international arms trade or on trade generally, or on the use of the 'global commons', such as the oceans or the sea-bed, or a progressive, GNP-related 'international tax'. Such devices reflect an ideal of cooperation among nations. The pendulum of internationalism has swung rather a long way from this ideal. The opposite of idealism is defeatism. We do not accept defeat; we hope others do not either.

Law of the Sea

One part of this international revenue generation was less futuristic than the rest: that which was to come from the Law of the Sea. The signing of the Convention on the Law of the Sea in Jamaica by 119 countries in December 1982 was an event of major international importance.

The treaty provides for ordering the uses of the sea and its resources, including such matters as rights of navigation, national exclusive economic zones, fishing, settlement of international disputes, and the mining of deep sea-bed minerals.

Twenty-five years have been spent in negotiations to construct a uniform legal framework for an area which comprises 71 per cent of the earth's surface and is man's greatest resource of the future. The broad questions with a North–South dimension concern: who exploits the oceans, how they exploit them, to whom they are responsible, who controls the regulatory agency, and the relationship between ocean- and land-based mineral producers.

The Convention establishes new forms of scientific and industrial cooperation between North and South and serves to ensure for all parties a secure and ordered oceans regime with a manageable framework for the efficient conservation and utilisation of the resources of the sea, such as oil, minerals and fish.

With the establishment of the Preparatory Committee, which will begin its work on 15 March 1983, the Conference on the Law of the Sea has in fact created an international interim regime for ocean exploration, and research and development in ocean mining technology which may adjust the ideas and ideals of the 1970s to the economic realities of the 1980s, and which, if properly utilised and fully supported, will be equally beneficial for developed and developing countries.

It is clearly in the interests of all nations to sign this Convention. The countries which do not lend their support to the treaty forfeit a secure and stable atmosphere which the treaty is intended to provide. The Commission urges those nations which have temporarily set themselves apart from the world community on this issue to make strenuous efforts to reconsider their positions and to sign the treaty as soon as possible within the two-year limit provided. An early acceptance of the treaty by these nations will ensure their participation in the work of the Preparatory Commission, which will act as the tool for further modification and compromise. The broad purposes of the treaty must be secured in its intended spirit; thereby a solid basis for the development of international cooperation will be created.

3 Trade

We have two kinds of concerns about trade: what is happening to the world's trading system; and what is happening to trade itself. The trading system is in a critical state. Its openness and orderliness have been substantially eroded in the last few years; a few more hard blows and it could collapse into the anarchy last seen in the 1930s. The GATT was designed to forestall a relapse into such a state; but many of its rules no longer prevail, and many new features of trade have arisen which neither the GATT nor other bodies cope with adequately. As has been said, an open trading system is like a bicycle; it must keep moving forward in order to stay upright. We discuss here some measures to promote that forward motion.

Secondly, world trade is stagnating. This is destructive for the industrial countries, for whom trade has always been a 'handmaiden of growth' and a means of facilitating an efficient international structure of production. For developing countries it is disastrous, as it severely damages their ability to transform their economies and to mobilise foreign capital and pay for essential imports.

Third World exports: a retrospective glance
The trade record of developing countries can be stated quite starkly. Those which were significant exporters of manufactures, or had well-diversified agricultural exports, had export growth in the 1970s only a little slower than in the 1960s; despite increasing protection in their markets, they increased their penetration, if at a diminishing rate.

For many others, the growth of exports lacked buoyancy because of generally weak demand for commodities and difficulties in securing market access for labour-intensive manufactures. Countries dependent on a small number of primary commodities suffered especially badly from the recession.

Thus the volume of merchandise exports from the middle-income countries (excluding the oil-exporters) grew at an average annual rate of 6.3 per cent in the 1960s and 4.4 per cent in the 1970s, whereas for the low-income countries (excluding China and India) growth was 5.3 per cent in the 1960s and *−1.1 per cent* in the 1970s. Of the World Bank's 36 low-income countries, 17 had *declining* exports in the 1970s; so too had 8 of the 20 middle-income countries just above the dividing line between low- and middle-income.

Viewed in another way, only $3 billion of the $226 billion increase in exports of developing countries over the 1970s (valued in the prices of their imports from OECD) were won by the low-income oil importers, whereas the middle-income group gained $118 billion and the oil-exporting countries (excluding the capital surplus ones) $105 billion.[31]

The more recent trading experience of developing countries has been depressing in general and disastrous in particular cases. With the sharp slow-down in the world economy, the increase in the volume of exports from developing countries (excluding OPEC) fell from 9½ per cent in 1979 to 5½ per cent in 1980 and under 4 per cent in 1981; with OPEC included the change would be even more marked, the volume of oil exports from this group of countries having fallen by around 10 per cent in 1980 and 18 per cent in 1981. The drop in prices of primary commodities exported by developing countries has been particularly severe (13 per cent in dollar terms for non-fuel products in 1981); prices of many of these commodities in real terms are now at the lowest level since the Second World War. Those of manufactures, however, have remained firm, with the

102

result that there has been a marked deterioration in the terms of trade of oil-importing developing countries, which declined at an average annual rate of 19 per cent in real terms between the last quarter of 1980 and the first of 1982. The effects have varied from one country to another, but most have suffered – not only the oil-importing middle-income countries, but the poorer countries as well. Malawi, for example, which had had a reasonably successful growth record for exports in the 1970s (at an average annual rate of 4.6 per cent), lost 20 per cent of its export earnings in the eighteen months up to mid-1982 due to the falling prices of its main commodity exports.

Having stagnated in volume during 1981, world trade in 1982 will almost certainly have fallen. Again the developing countries have been particularly badly hit, with exports from the fast growing exporters of manufactures (the newly industrialising countries) being among those which have suffered from contracting markets caused by the recession and a tightening of protective measures. Moreover, prospects for developing countries' export growth in the next few years are not bright, and there is little or no indication that the poorer countries will not continue to be left behind, as they were in the 1970s.

Trade among developing countries, or 'South–South trade', is not drawing in poorer countries either. In general, whether in manufactures, processed primary products or primary commodities themselves, the better-off developing countries were capturing most of the growth, when there was any, and the poorer countries were going backwards. Now that trade is generally stagnant, almost all countries are suffering, the poorest most of all.

Commodities
As already noted, recent years have been disastrous for commodity exporters and there is not much to report on action towards remedies. Market prices are still largely unstable. There has been little progress on establishing the Common Fund. To date less than forty countries have

103

ratified the agreement. There is also little progress towards new International Commodity Agreements (ICAs) for individual commodities. And the export earnings stabilisation arrangements in existence – the IMF Compensatory Financing Facility and STABEX under the Lomé Convention – make very inadequate provision for compensation.

We continue to support the establishment of market stabilisation arrangements. For various well-known reasons connected both with the nature of the products and with the manner in which their production, trade and distribution is organised, international prices of commodities entering into world trade have continued to fluctuate widely and sharply. Even on the basis of annual averages, the IMF price index of foodstuffs fell 14 per cent in 1981 and is projected (by the IMF) to decline 16 per cent in 1982,[32] this following a 34-per-cent rise in 1980. Fluctuations for individual commodities have been much greater. Between June 1980 and June 1982, for example, the price of sugar (outside special arrangements) fell 78 per cent, rubber by 37 per cent and copper by 35 per cent. Such fluctuations cause developing countries producing these commodities considerable macro-economic problems. But in so far as price instability can adversely affect consumers and importers as well as producers and exporters, both sides of the trade have an interest in stabilisation. Yet little of substance has been achieved by way of institutional arrangements.

The urgency of the present situation for developing countries lies essentially in the precipitate manner in which prices and values of their commodity exports have fallen. There is evidence for some commodities that volumes of consumption have not declined a great deal during the recession, however, and that price falls may have had more to do with supply increases. If this is so, then for non-perishable commodities greater attention should be given to stock-building, nationally or internationally, within or outside ICAs. But for this to be successful, greatly increased finance would have to be forthcoming. The IMF has some capacity to finance commodity stocks under the Buffer Stock Facility – but only in the case of commodities governed by ICAs. Consuming countries would presumably dislike supply control outside ICAs, though in the absence of adequate international market stabilisation arrangements, this would seem to be justified. The early establishment of the Common Fund would be of great assistance to the setting up and functioning of buffer stock ICAs. We strongly urge countries which have not done so to ratify the agreement so that the Fund could become operational as early as possible.

The principal alternative to stabilising and improving prices through supply controls (which eventually means production controls) is compensation for reduced export earnings. The Report discussed reasons why doing so is not a complete alternative; but it accepted the objective, and recommended considerable enlargement and improvement of the IMF Compensatory Financing Facility, which we have already discussed under 'Finance' in Chapter 2.

Solutions have to be found urgently to the severe problems caused by the continuing slump in primary product prices if the deprivation and hardship already experienced by poor countries is not to be exacerbated further. In the light of these disturbing trends, commodity stabilisation arrangements should be reviewed with the aim of increasing their coverage and effectiveness. In addition greater provision should be made for compensation under the IMF Compensatory Financing Facility so that compensation could be more closely related to the extent of export shortfalls. One route which we believe deserves increased attention is the possible combination of commodity price and earnings stabilisation arrangements with long-term supply guarantees or the command over future supplies as collateral for short-term price guarantees.

Trade in agricultural commodities
Apart from problems of fluctuating prices, exporters in developing countries face difficulties as a result of the nature of the agricultural policies in their main markets. The EEC, Japan and, to a lesser extent, the United States all protect their domestic agriculture from competing imports – butter, oilseed, wheat, maize, rice, sugar, beef and tobacco are the main objects of this protection. As far as developing countries are concerned, protective measures on wheat and beef principally affect the exports of Argentina, while those on the remaining products affect a number of countries. And it is not only export markets in the protecting countries which are restricted; subsidised exports hurt developing countries' exports to other markets. Subsidised EEC sugar exports rose to 18.3 per cent of the world market in 1981.

Agricultural products which Northern countries cannot produce face few tariff barriers in their raw state; but processed products are a different story. Both mineral and agricultural raw materials do face a variety of non-tariff barriers. There are still some high tariffs, however, mainly in order to protect preferential suppliers (for example the ACP countries' exports to the EEC), but partly for revenue raising purposes. East European countries also restrict entry in order to achieve bilateral balancing of trade, and the opening up of the markets of these countries would have a significant effect in enlarging world import demand for tropical products.

Processed commodities
The extent of protection on processing is a major obstacle to development in the Third World, whose natural path of industrialisation would be in many cases to move from exporting products in primary form to those processed at various 'higher' levels, closer to the finished article as purchased for final consumption. According to a UNIDO study, developing countries could earn an extra $44 billion (gross) per annum if their exports of seven major minerals

had been taken up to the metal bar stage.[33] Large gains would also be possible if tariffs on processed agricultural goods were removed: a 20-per-cent increase in value-added by developing countries on eight commodities alone, according to a World Bank estimate.[34]

Yet it is just such progress that protection prevents. The rates of effective tariff protection are well over 100 per cent on several products in the EEC and Japan, rather lower in the US (mostly below 30 per cent). The tariffs escalate with the degree of processing. And a barrage of non-tariff measures impede processed exports. Among the most notorious of these measures are the excise taxes imposed for revenue purposes on tea and coffee, in the Federal Republic of Germany for example. There are few trade reforms of more importance to developing countries, especially the poorer among them, than the removal of these types of barriers.

Manufactures

When it comes to manufactures, the 'new protection' is in place side by side with the old: subsidies and government procurement, other non-tariff measures, and tariffs which are in most cases higher than average on products of export interest to developing countries. And protection has been worsening. The proportion of OECD imports of manufactures controlled by non-tariff measures was put at 17 per cent in 1980 compared with only 4 per cent in 1974. And it is worse for developing countries' manufactures; 30 per cent of these exports to OECD were thus controlled in 1979 compared with only 11 per cent in the case of OECD intra-trade.

A significant and growing proportion of trade in manufactures takes place on a basis which is not governed by the principles and rules of the GATT but is on a bilateral, discriminatory and non-transparent basis. This administered or managed trade, where discretion rather than rules prevails, is not only very difficult to monitor and assess but almost invariably means that the weakest lose the most. The resulting increase in uncertainty of market access has not only inhibited and distorted trade but has adversely affected investment. In the words of the report of the Commonwealth Expert Group on Protectionism: 'Uncertainties, by influencing trade and investment decisions, generate the very conditions which make for still greater encroachments upon liberalised trade and thus breed further uncertainties in an ever-intensifying downward spiral.'[35]

In addition to the trade distortions caused by barriers to market access and subsidies to exports, an underlying factor which has become important recently in the pressures for increased protectionism has been the lack of coordination of monetary policies. The speed and extent of interest rate fluctuations, and the consequent expansion of differentials between countries, have led to marked increases in exchange rate movements. This has exaggerated the undervaluation and overvaluation of currencies and has artificially affected competitiveness between countries, thus encouraging resort to protectionism by those whose exports are adversely affected.

These exchange rate movements have also magnified trade imbalances between particular countries and the concomitant tendency to seek bilateral balancing, especially in trade with Japan. While recognising that bilateral reciprocity has value as a bargaining device to secure improved access in protected markets, we regard the spread of this phenomenon (previously restricted to relatively few countries, especially in Eastern Europe) as a dangerous development. Multilateral balancing is the only way to seek a recovery of world trade.

Costs of protection

Protective measures are costly not only for the potential exporters to the countries which employ them, but also for the protecting countries themselves. Very commonly an import barrier protects a relatively small number of workers in an industry and penalises a much larger number of consumers or other industrial producers who have to pay higher prices than they would if the article were imported freely. The costs to those workers, if rendered redundant, would be concentrated and thus visible, while the costs borne by others because of protection, even if much larger in total, are widely spread.

When governments yield to protectionist pressures they rarely calculate their cost. While it is difficult to reflect all elements in cost estimates, especially during a recession when resources are unemployed, the orders of magnitude shown in studies which have been done are instructive. One study looked at just five items in the USA between 1975-77: carbon steel, footwear, sugar, meat and television sets. Keeping out imports of these items cost consumers $4 billion, which worked out at $50,000 for each job protected in the industries making them. And this was in a period when US employment was rising rapidly. The cost of protection in the Canadian clothing industry in 1979 was $33,000 per job – when the average wage in the industry was $10,000 per job. The EEC's Common Agricultural Policy (CAP) was reckoned to cost consumers $4 billion above world prices in 1978 (though that figure would have to be reduced if the price effects of the Community's buying in world markets were allowed for). One authority has been led to ask whether 'the Community has a future as a machine for redistributing self-inflicted losses'.[36] Though the above examples all refer to developed countries, similar costs are borne by consumers in some of the more advanced developing countries which continue protection and do not allow infant industries to grow up.

Taxpayers' costs for subsidies to industries facing foreign competition are similarly enormous. And to these direct and measurable costs must be added all the others due to thwarted competition and its long-run effects on growth and efficiency; not least the failure of exports to rise because other countries, faced by loss of markets due to protection, cannot earn the foreign exchange to buy them.

Such are the ramifications and perversities of protection. Often the difficulties are greater than the above calculations suggest. Very frequently industries, labour unions or large corporations succeed in persuading governments to protect them at a cost to the rest of society which, if those who had to pay it were equally well organised, might be exposed as excessive. This can generate foreign retaliation and a downward spiral of 'beggar-thy-neighbour' policies. Taking into account the direct, indirect and dynamic effects of protection, the costs to society are thus enormous. Even employment effects are usually negative. The example of the 1930s is a reminder of the dangers.

Reversing protectionism
In times of recession it is harder for governments to resist protectionism; they can see no new jobs for displaced workers to move to. But even in a recession such action is misguided as it will simply reduce specialisation on the basis of comparative advantage and will thus further lower income below its full potential. We believe it is essential that the world's major trading nations make a determined effort to stop moving in the dangerous direction they have taken in their trade actions and policies.

No one expects that protection is going to disappear, at least in the foreseeable future. But it is possible to make it more transparent and predictable and in other ways to minimise its damage. The international trading system can and must be made subject to internationally agreed rules. The impact of increasing disorder on the trade of developing countries has recently been comprehensively examined in the report of the Commonwealth Expert Group already cited. The report provides good guidance on the trade reforms required. There are a number of areas in which we believe *a renewed commitment is urgently needed to enforce the disciplines of an open trading system governed by multilateral agreements.*

110

Immediate priorities

First, however, we make a few introductory remarks on our view of the immediate priorities which need to be followed if the present emergency is to be overcome. An effective safeguards mechanism and the need to restrict and reduce the so-called grey areas is perhaps the most immediate issue to tackle, although the need to start the process of incorporating agriculture into the GATT system and to formulate more effective dispute settlement procedures is also urgent. Overlaying these specific issues, however, is the necessity to keep up the pressure on governments to reinforce their commitment to resist protectionism, and to be in a position to begin the process of reducing it when recovery makes this feasible. In the light of these priorities we broadly agree with the timetable proposed by the recent Ministerial Meeting of GATT. At the same time we must register our own disappointment at the meagre results of that Meeting which meant the loss of a great opportunity. Whether the undertaking given to hold the line on protectionism will succeed against mounting domestic pressures remains to be seen. In this connection the recent steps taken by the US and EEC to avoid a trade war over the issue of agricultural export subsidies is to be welcomed.

Principles and rules

An essential basis for reforming the trading system must be the principles and rules it observes. Greater transparency and predictability would ensure that all parties – including the public at large – know precisely what the rules are. Many crucial parts of the existing rules are subject to procedures secluded from the public gaze, or so ill-defined that countries can practically do as they wish. There is urgent need for every country to be much more transparent in the manner in which it imposes trade restrictions, including subsidies and other trade distorting measures, so that a wider and more representative range of national and international interests can be heard and taken into account. This would provide the opportunity to assess the effects of such actions on domestic consumers (final or intermediate), the overall impact on the national economy, and the likely effect on overseas suppliers, including possible retaliatory action.

Non-discrimination is another key principle which has been substantially and increasingly breached, especially in trade relations with developing countries. In the meantime the conditions of special treatment for developing countries, without which the difficulties of the low-income countries we described above cannot be redressed, are not being honoured. Such 'special treatment' is enshrined in the articles of the GATT, but it has been increasingly infringed in recent years by demands for reciprocity in trade negotiations and in the codes established to control non-tariff measures.

Safeguards

At the core of an approach to current trade problems must be a revised 'safeguards code'. The current Article XIX of the GATT is supposed to delimit the circumstances in which countries can legitimately resort to protection, usually of a quantitative nature, when their domestic producers are threatened. They would be permitted to do this when 'serious injury' was likely; originally it was intended that action would be subject to prior consultation, and would not discriminate among supplying countries. But these provisions of the Article have been avoided by the mass of 'voluntary export restraints' and 'orderly marketing arrangements' of recent years.

A new safeguards code would need to define what constituted 'serious injury' (as Article XIX at present does not) according to economic criteria; the importing country would be required to demonstrate the causal link between the allegedly disruptive imports and the 'injury'. The code would also need to define the limited period for which protection would be permitted, and appropriate international surveillance. Ideally the code should also continue to be non-discriminatory; that is, it would not permit an importing country to be selective about the countries from which imports would be affected. This has been among the most contentious issues, however, and though the developing countries have generally continued to oppose selectivity, mindful of their experience with the Multi-Fibre Arrangement, certain among them have emphasised that non-discrimination would in some cases harm 'innocent' parties.

The Multi-Fibre Arrangement (MFA) which controls trade in textiles and clothing is, from the developing countries' point of view, perhaps the worst example of the current array of protective measures. It is of course a sector where the developed countries have great difficulties, often with large numbers of ill-paid workers in older industrial areas, but unable to compete internationally. A satisfactory safeguards code would subsume the MFA and a large range of other protective measures and would facilitate their being phased out. It would have to be supported by positive adjustment measures in the importing countries, so that temporary protection under its provisions could be removed without economic disruption. Protection under the safeguard code should be allowed only after a careful review which hears representation from all the parties affected and takes into account all interests. *We strongly urge a renewed and determined commitment to establish a revised safeguard code as early as possible,* and hope to see early and substantive progress emanating from the negotiations to be undertaken within GATT to formulate a comprehensive understanding before the 1983 session of the Contracting Parties.

Agricultural protection

A second main area where progress is needed is in trade in agricultural commodities. There is no good reason for this large-scale exemption from the provisions of the GATT. The difficulties, however, are so intractable that one could not imagine movement forward being made on all fronts simultaneously. A start could be made with a commitment not to introduce any new measures or increase any existing ones, which have been designed explicitly for protective purposes; then agricultural support measures and subsidies to exports could be tackled under a new code of international principles; and agricultural surpluses, which disrupt international markets and are not required to provide food reserves, should be reduced and access to markets gradually improved

Processed products, manufactures and services

We would urge the drawing up of a programme to phase out tariff-escalation for processed primary products. On other manufactures where tariffs are still significant, they should be most reduced on products of interest to developing country exporters in future multilateral negotiations. Preferential schemes, where they exist, should be made free of limitations which hurt the export prospects of developing countries, especially the poorest ones. We have not discussed trade in services separately, but this is an area of growing importance, and of trade restrictions. Analysis by international agencies is needed to see how best this trade may be brought into negotiation and itself placed under rules which take into account its special circumstances.

New GATT codes

The 1973 'Tokyo Round' of GATT negotiations established new codes on non-tariff measures. The usefulness of the codes depends mainly on the willingness of governments to make them effective. This is especially true in the case of Northern governments, but it is also important for more Southern governments to become signatories of the codes and thereby accept the obligations as well as the rights they confer. All the codes are important. From the developing countries' point of view the most important are those on subsidies to domestic production, countervailing duties, and on government procurement, which seek to regulate governments' ability to distort international competition by means which the original GATT rules do not cover. There are still ambiguities and escape routes for developed countries in the codes, which can affect developing countries' trade severely. *We recommend the continuing improvement of these codes, incorporating more precise rules and stricter disciplines, and paying greater attention to the interests and circumstances of developing countries.*

Dispute settlement

There is at present no satisfactory machinery for settling disputes in international trade. This is in part because the rules themselves are not sufficiently well defined. But such dispute settlement procedures as there are lack transparency; that is, they are not open to public scrutiny; they lack powers to ensure compliance from transgressors after arbitration is made; and they are excessively concerned with achieving bilateral accommodation. We would propose that stronger mechanisms of dispute settlement be established so as to ensure that all member countries comply with their decisions. A little progress on this was made by the 1982 GATT Ministerial Meeting which agreed on means to make more effective use of the existing mechanisms and on specific improvements in the conciliation procedures.

Institutions

For the international trading system to become more open and to operate on agreed rules, it is essential that GATT should become more universally acceptable. At present developing countries do not feel that their interests are adequately represented in GATT. In part they themselves have not made sufficient efforts to try to ensure that it does so; in part the industrial countries neglect the GATT themselves, resorting to consultations within the OECD and thus weakening the GATT machinery. But in part also, the coverage of the GATT has left a vacuum in the treatment of issues, which have had to be taken up by other institutions, most notably UNCTAD. And in many fields the effects on other countries' exports of national policies towards agriculture or industry are as important as those on trade policy itself. There is a clear need for closer consultation and cooperation between GATT, UNCTAD, IMF and other international bodies, and for more joint and coordinated efforts in their activities. Over time the functions of GATT and UNCTAD should be encompassed in one organisation – an International Trade Organisation – as we recommended in our Report. With proper consultation, international issues relating to the nexus between trade and financial policies (which affect exchange rates), on structural adjustment and protection and national policies could all be analysed and discussed, leading to more fruitful negotiations on the parts to be played by appropriate agencies.

The recent GATT Ministerial Meeting demonstrated how far apart the various sides are in their positions on a number of vital issues. In view of this, *we believe it would be valuable if a high level and representative international group could confer and discuss how progress could best be made.* There is already a Consultative Group of 18 within the GATT; but wider and more powerful representation is desirable, possibly at Ministerial level. Such a group could make proposals on trade in the same manner as did the Group of 20 on international monetary issues. It could well take as part of its agenda the recommendations in the report of the Commonwealth Expert Group already referred to, to which we subscribe. There are enough well-reasoned recommendations and studies for any amount of substantial progress to be made. The problem is to have them moved forward by constructive negotiation. For that it is necessary to have a degree of prior international accord on specific issues and a greater willingness on the part of all countries to yield some degree of national autonomy in policy-making.

Other initiatives

Our preoccupation has been – as anyone's must be – with the world trading system and its central international institutions. But there is much which could be done even without full international agreement. Many countries could improve their own policies, to their own and their trading partners' benefit. The EEC has to do something about its agricultural policies, for example; the huge surpluses it piles up and their disposal are an embarrassment to Europe's politicians, and a costly one. The EEC Commission has itself already proposed reforms for the CAP. But more determined efforts must be made.

Much more could also be done to extend public awareness of the real costs of protection. In some countries trade restrictions have to pass far more public scrutiny than in others: thus protection cannot usually be increased without a public enquiry at which all parties can state their case; reports of the enquiries are published and decisions widely publicised. Similar arrangements should be encouraged elsewhere. GATT, UNCTAD and the IMF all monitor trade barriers; more publicity for the results of their investigations would make surveillance more effective.

South–South cooperation

Finally there are opportunities for more cooperation in trade among developing countries, as our Report described. The possibility of low growth rates and of continuing protection in the developed countries increases the need for such cooperation. Regional cooperation is one field. Experience in the 1960s was not very favourable, but more recently the Association of South East Asian Nations has made significant advances, and there are promising developments in Western and Southern Africa and the Caribbean Community. The reduction of trade barriers by developing countries, perhaps initially in the form of trade preferences for other developing countries, is a vital step in promoting South–South trade, as is credit and payments cooperation discussed under 'Finance' in Chapter 2. The more advanced developing countries should give priority in their trade liberalisation to the interests of the poorer countries. There is also scope for developing countries to establish transnational marketing and purchasing enterprises to reduce dependence on Northern corporations and facilitate trade expansion.

4 Food and Energy

Food and energy are increasingly related. As energy prices rise, so do the costs of imports and direct use of energy in agriculture, and hence food becomes more expensive. For most developing countries both food and fuel weigh heavily in imports. Those with limited domestic fuel resources may find themselves faced with the choice between using scarce land for food or for energy-yielding vegetation. And poor people in developing countries are being forced into the exploitation of tree cover for fuelwood, with consequential destruction of the ecological base for agriculture. Major investments and research will be necessary, and concerted action, to secure compatible increases in production and consumption of both energy and food.

Food

Millions of people in the Third World do not eat enough. It is a fact unbearable to contemplate. But the principal condition for an end to hunger is that those who do not eat enough should have the incomes to buy adequate food or the means to produce it: an end to hunger differs only in degree from an end to poverty. And that in turn encompasses practically everything in this document, from the international measures which would provide a more favourable external environment for development, to action by national leaders, governments and people in developing countries to ensure that development reaches the poor. Considerable progress has been made in some countries. The North could help with trade and aid policies that are more sensitive to the urgent need to expand food production in the South. What has to be done to end hunger is vast. Yet sometimes it seems that even the unheroic steps that could considerably improve the situation will not be taken.

Ensuring that if the incomes were there, enough food would be available for them to be spent on is also a major but more manageable task. Some developing countries already generate food surpluses in some years, yet people without adequate purchasing power still go hungry. The government could in principle pay for the difference between the high price needed to persuade the farmer to produce the food and the low price the poor could afford – but where there is mass poverty, it may not be able to raise enough in taxes to cover that gap for all the poor. In other countries food has to be imported just to meet the prevailing inadequate levels of effective demand. For some of them the current balance of payments squeeze makes even those amounts of imports an impossible burden.

Moving on both fronts – to ensure both adequate incomes and adequate food supplies – in fact requires action in closely related areas. The bulk of the poor are in rural areas where the increased food volumes must be grown. Employment-creating agricultural development is the key to growth in low-income countries. Even in the faster growing countries agricultural progress has usually lain behind the success of manufacturing, as it did in the eighteenth- and nineteenth-century growth of countries now industrialised. Manufacturing cannot be ignored; urban jobs have to be provided too, and only manufacturing can generate really rapid growth. But many countries have suffered from premature attempts to industrialise.

Food deficits in Africa

The worst of today's food problems are in Africa, mainly Sub-Saharan Africa. Many of the problems stem from climate and soil conditions. But many African governments have also devoted only a slender proportion of their budgets to agriculture. They have frequently allowed procurement prices of government purchasing agencies to go too low, and exchange rates too high, to leave farmers with adequate production incentives. Research into improved crop varieties and growing methods has been insufficient. Foreign aid donors have taken a long time to understand how to help small-scale farming, and have too often supported large-scale schemes with limited impact on food production. Food-aid has sometimes been unhelpful; but this is mainly because of the way it has been used. Ensuring that small farmers and the landless have adequate access to land can be crucial in facilitating food production.

In recent times however the external situation has itself contributed to the poor performance of agriculture. The shortage of foreign exchange has limited the availability of imported fertilisers, pesticides, farm-implements and spares, fuel for irrigation pumps and tractors. In the poorest countries budgets are so tight that governments have difficulty even paying salaries of extension workers, or ensuring that their vehicles are fuelled and maintained. In these conditions more 'aid for agriculture' in the traditional form of agricultural projects will not be sufficient. It is why we have repeatedly stressed the necessity for programme aid, for aid to cover local-cost and recurrent expenditures – without them agriculture will not receive vital assistance in the appropriate form.

There is already a deteriorating food situation in Africa: food production not keeping pace with population growth, and growing dependence on food imports. In the 1960s African food production grew by 2.6 per cent and in the 1970s, by 1.6 per cent a year: in *per capita* terms that is 0.1-per-cent annual growth in the 1960s, and 1.1-per-cent annual *decline* in the 1970s. In the last decade, wars, political upheavals and civil strife as well as acute drought have contributed to the downward trend in several countries.

African countries on average are importing 8–9 per cent of their food. This is a sad state of affairs for countries with typically two thirds or more of their labour engaged in agriculture. The imports are part consequence and part cause of declining production – overvalued exchange rates making imports cheaper than they should be. And the countries cannot pay even for those imports; in Africa on average 20 per cent of cereal imports are covered by food-aid; for low-income Africa the figure is over 40 per cent. This too is in some ways aggravating the situation, since imports of wheat and rice have been growing the fastest (11 per cent a year in the 1970s), partly supported by food-aid, and encouraging consumption habits, in urban areas especially, which could not easily be met by local production. Wheat can often only be grown in tropical Africa at very great expense, and in some countries rice too; so once the taste for them is ingrained, it cannot be satisfied by domestic production.

Other countries, including some in South Asia, have also had difficult food problems. Developing countries are the biggest importers of food grains – mostly the middle-income countries, which took 36 per cent of world grain imports in 1980.[37] Even among the countries which can pay for large imports there are several which should be producing more of their own food; where oil or other mineral exports dominate the exchange rate, agriculture has often been adversely affected. There have also been 'success' stories: India and China among them. Even Bangladesh moved from the critical shortage years of 1973-75 into a more comfortable situation later in the decade; however, its long-term food problem appears extremely difficult with its high population density and population due to double in less than thirty years.

Long-term prospects

The long-term prospects for developing countries generally are indeed worrying: if present production trends continue they are, in the FAO's words, 'alarming'. To maintain present inadequate levels of demand, imports of cereals would have to rise from an average 36.4 million tonnes in 1978-79 to 72 million in 1990 and 132 million tonnes by the end of the century; for the poorer countries the amounts involved would be far in excess of their capacity to pay. The appalling growth in the numbers of malnourished people, the degree of dependence on imports, the sheer physical problems of transporting such volumes of grain, the financial implications all add up to a situation which would be 'politically and economically unacceptable'.[38]

This long-term outlook if trends continue, the already heavy balance of payments burden of food imports, the need to give agriculture its proper place in the growth process, the deteriorating food situation in several countries, and the need to create more employment, have all combined in recent years to give a new urgency to raising food and agricultural production. Not least in Africa, where the 1980 Lagos Plan of Action set a target for the 1980s of tripling the growth rates of the 1970s. That plan will call for considerable outside assistance. Yet the African countries, which have adopted the plan, have not yet received any additional help.

Cooperation since 1980

Despite the recognition of needs by policy-makers of North and South and the urgency of action, cooperation efforts have been wholly insufficient. A major meeting on food of OECD aid donors in the Development Assistance Committee (DAC) in March 1981 noted that aid for food and agriculture from DAC members, OPEC, and the multilateral institutions doubled in real terms during 1973-79 but growth slowed down between 1978-79 and did not rise further (in real terms) in 1980, official commitments by donor groups in that year reaching some

$11 billion. Aid for food and agriculture as a proportion of total aid represented about one quarter of official commitments by all donor groups. It has stagnated since.

Obstacles to aid increases included delays in payment of contributions to IDA, budgetary restrictions, lack of firms and personnel capable of supplying equipment and required services in countries offering tied aid, the unstable political situation in some recipient countries, and the 'tendency to lay greater stress on (other) sectors (e.g. energy and raw materials)'. The DAC donors put emphasis – as did the Cancun Summit and the European Commission's proposal to be discussed below – on national commitment to food strategies by recipients. About fifty developing countries have in fact prepared or are preparing such strategies. But the pressures on aid to agriculture have been disturbing: even within the non-increasing aid total, project assistance has been moving to cash crops for export away from food production.

IFAD
There can be some satisfaction in the recent agreement to replenish IFAD's funds. It has received pledges on a broad international basis, including $450 million from OPEC countries. IFAD, the International Fund for Agricultural Development, has on the whole had a good record of imaginative agricultural projects with particular attention to reaching the poor. It has kept administrative costs down by hiring consultants for many purposes rather than permanent staff. And it has proved successful as an organisation with a voting structure giving balanced representation to OPEC countries, other developing countries and the North. Yet at the end of 1982 the US contribution still awaited Congressional approval, without which other countries' contributions were put in doubt.

New initiatives
There are new initiatives in various quarters. For example, the Commission of the European Communities has

proposed a Plan of Action to Combat World Hunger, which has already won support from Canada and other non-Community countries. The plan has several components:

- Action to support national policies for developing the agricultural sector, implemented by developing countries which wish to join their own efforts with donors' assistance in national food strategies.
- Projects or programmes to assist regional groups of countries coping with common difficulties such as ecological deterioration or other obstacles to the development of productive resources.
- Measures to increase the external food security of developing countries, and in particular special efforts to mitigate the consequences of current food deficits in the poorest countries, including ensuring that the International Emergency Reserve has adequate resources.

This plan has a great deal in common with the recommendations of our Emergency Programme. Action along these lines deserves broad support. In particular, the proposal to cooperate with countries pursuing national food strategies has a number of virtues. It takes account of the need to rationalise the use of different elements of assistance – financial aid, technical cooperation, food-aid – in collaboration with a coherent national strategy to move towards food self-sufficiency. Community arrangements are already in hand to pursue this approach with three countries: Kenya, Mali and Zambia.

Assistance for food production
This plan is so far envisaged only on a relatively modest scale. Adequately financed and greatly extended, it could form a set of organising principles for a wider programme of North–South cooperation. To support the fifty countries now preparing national food strategies – those which need external support – would require the increases

in bilateral and multilateral assistance proposed in this document, and within expanded aid totals, a major strengthening of assistance to agriculture.

Different countries need different degrees of support. For the poorest countries, the preparation of a food strategy is likely to require technical assistance; it has to be part of an agricultural strategy, indeed a development strategy, which may not exist in any articulated form. And its implementation, with everything it calls for in terms of administrative and technical manpower, will need advances in training and education. As was noted above, far from pursuing any bold new food strategy, the poorest countries are prevented by the present external economic crisis even from carrying out day-to-day tasks which have hitherto been within their means. It should not be imagined that there is a fast route to food self-sufficiency in these circumstances.

Halting and reversing ecological degradation

Growing pressure on land, increasing use of chemicals, desertification and deforestation are reducing the productivity of soils in many parts of the world. The removal of forest cover, incautious use of chemicals and fertilisers, and soil erosion are destroying the soils and agricultural potential of scarce land resources and causing severe environmental damage. The FAO estimates that as much as a quarter of total farmland in developing countries will require soil and water conservation measures by the end of the century. At a cost of $100 per hectare, and $500 where flood control is needed, such measures could by themselves cost well over $25 billion over the rest of the century.[39] There is an enormous need here for both national and regional planning, research and cooperation – much of which, as already noted, must be considered in close relation to energy use and development. *We emphasise the need for resources to halt and reverse these processes of ecological degradation, which now assume emergency proportions.*

Research

A particular need is for increased support to research – particularly for Africa where the greatest need is for *adaptive* research, to discover which crop varieties and farming techniques are most suitable in local conditions. And generally for all agriculture in developing countries research must find new methods of production which are less vulnerable to the high cost of energy.

There continues to be an immense need for food crop research carried out within the indigenous conditions of the developing countries themselves. Such research should be dedicated to improved crop varieties, animal breeds, and farming techniques most suitable to local conditions. Carried out by local researchers, the efforts would as well considerably enhance local and regional research competence and capacity.

The magnitude of returns on research expenditure and the close connection between research and increased yields have both been irrefutably demonstrated. While there have been considerable strides in international support for developing-country agricultural research in recent years, the commitment to research and the funds available both appear to be stagnating. Governments of developing countries must also make greater provision. They should not be put off by the tendency of results to be indirect and to take time to come to fruition.

Considerable needs remain unmet. One may deplore the stagnation of aid to agriculture; but there one is talking of very large amounts of aid. For research it is a question of programmes costing tens of millions of dollars, not billions. Not to produce these relatively modest sums is reprehensible neglect.

Food security

One area where thinking has changed since the publication of the Report is on the desirable size of international and national food stocks. Recent work, as already noted, suggests that countries can rely on trade to make up

127

deficits to a greater extent than was once thought safe. The events of the early 1970s which made such reliance seem dangerous are now considered to be rather unlikely to recur. But some countries' needs for security measures are greater than others'. Sizeable stocks are still considered necessary for security and stability; the other complement to reliance on trade must be a food import financing facility. Such a facility would compensate countries faced with a combination of greater-than-normal food import bills and smaller-than-normal export earnings. As noted, the IMF's CFF has in fact been extended to cover cereal import requirements and goes part of the way towards meeting the problem. But the coverage is very limited and it needs more resources for this purpose, as well as for others. Greater freedom of trade in food, as we describe elsewhere, would also help price stability and supplies.

On international measures of food security the history of negotiations has been unsatisfactory. The most recent attempts to conclude a new International Wheat Agreement (IWA) ended in deadlock towards the end of 1981, with failure to agree on the new proposals evolved in the previous year. These took account of the much wider price fluctuations which now characterise the world market, making agreement on price ranges very difficult. They retained the concept of internationally coordinated national stocks, but substituted consultations in situations of market stress for price-related automaticity in the operation of reserve stocks and other measures. The recent extension of the present IWA to June 1986 will of itself make no contribution to improving food security. It does not incorporate stabilisation mechanisms. Current expectations for world supplies are reasonably confident for the immediate period, but low prices threaten output in the future and progress is needed.

The continuing US objections seem to be resistance to relinquishing a part of the control of its own stocks to an international agreement, the current US administration being opposed to internationally managed stocks, and

128

holding to the view that a reserve system should be 'market-oriented'. But other factors have been (and may continue to be) important. In earlier negotiations developing countries objected to the high range of trigger prices proposed; neither then nor in the 1981 discussions did it seem that they received adequate supply assurances. Nor has there been any agreement within the context of the IWA to assist developing countries with their stockholding costs. A new IWA should provide both flexibility and firm assurances of supply.

International grain reserves are the measure *par excellence* where the possibilities of action without US cooperation are slender. The European Community could play a considerable role, together with Canada and Australia. If the US cannot be persuaded to support them in principle, at the very least it must continue to bear a major share of world grain stocks adequate to lend a degree of security to world markets, and be willing to use them to help stabilise markets and supply imports to deficit countries as need arises. Arguably it is in the US interest to play this part, rather than pursue short-run concerns and encourage other countries to believe it cannot be relied on. But *we urge continued pursuit of a new International Wheat Agreement with full international support.*

In 1981 the World Food Council made a new proposal for a developing-country-owned international grain reserve. Under this proposal, which is still in process of elaboration,[40] developing countries would hold their own grain stocks, receiving international assistance as necessary – which could include funding by the IMF's Buffer Stock Facility, provided the stocks formed part of a recognised international agreement.

There is increasing emphasis today on specific national and local aspects of food security. Stocks of grain in far-away places may not do much for the poor and hungry afflicted by local food scarcities and falls in income, unless logistics of transport and distribution are improved and timely food imports reach affected areas. Often

129

individuals' problems are due to *seasonal* variations in food supplies or in incomes. On-farm storage, storage at all levels, must be part of the solution; other 'local' aspects of combating hunger are: increasing food production on small landholdings; public works; small credit programmes; direct consumption subsidies; better focusing of food-aid; land reform and labour-intensive investments. Thus while we support a proposal along the lines of that of the World Food Council, we hope that as work on it proceeds it will take full account of the needs for infrastructural development and finance. And we recognise that its contributions to food security must be complemented by other measures in overall food and agricultural strategies.

Food-aid

Food-aid has become a vexed subject. Many commentators, observing its frequent defects, would like to see it abolished, or at least confined to emergency situations. Even the Cancun Summit expressed the latter view in its final communiqué – wrongly, in our opinion. Food-aid does indeed have defects, but they are mostly avoidable. Several countries have avoided them and made good use of food-aid in the past: they include Botswana, Colombia, India, Lesotho, Pakistan, Tunisia and Turkey. As long as there is political support in the donor countries for this form of aid, while appropriations for other aid face legislative struggles, food-aid must continue as a contribution to the poorer countries' nutritional and balance of payments needs. Its defects, where they occur, must be corrected.

The common criticisms of food-aid are that it acts as a disincentive to local food producers by bringing down food prices; that it reduces countries' commitment to agricultural development; that it does not reach the nutritionally deprived; and that it encourages consumption habits which cannot always be met in the course of time from domestic production. In recent times there have been

130

attempts to circumvent some of these problems by 'projectising' food-aid; that is, by using it as wages in development projects, or finance for them. Methods have also been found to distribute food-aid in ways which do not affect the prices farmers receive.

Professional opinion today recognises that the criticisms are valid for some recipient countries in some periods – but are false for others. If there have been countries where food-aid has weakened governments' determination to support agricultural development, that too is avoidable in the kind of policy dialogue between donors and recipients which takes place today. The idea that food and other aid should support national food strategies will make this more certain. If food-aid gets siphoned off to feed civil servants or soldiers rather than the poor and hungry – that is something wrong with the management of food-aid, not with the principle of it.

To those who argue that food-aid encourages a taste for food which cannot be produced locally, the reply is that many factors other than food-aid have discouraged the production, processing and marketing of domestically produced foods. This is, nevertheless, one of the stronger arguments for phasing out food-aid, to the extent that countries *can* approach self-sufficiency in domestically producible foods. But until that phasing-out can take place it is better that people eat the 'wrong' food than no food at all. Finally, there do seem to be many complaints about food-aid projects. But are they accurate? This is a subject that deserves further exploration, for certainly many food-for-work projects and other projects supported by food-aid have been successful. On all counts, everything depends on the policies of the recipient country and the availability of professional and administrative competence to carry them out. It is not food-aid that should be objected to, but poorly used food-aid.

A new Food Aid Convention was concluded in 1981, which raises guaranteed quantities of food aid from 4.2 to 7.6 million tonnes. This is a welcome if modest increase in the guaranteed amount. What is more important however is the food-aid target which has been set at 10 million tonnes since the World Food Conference in 1975 but has not yet been reached. *A new and much higher target is now needed. We also propose an international commitment to meet the agreed target of 500,000 tonnes for the Emergency Food Reserve on an annual basis* (so far it has only been achieved once, in 1981); and in view of increasing needs we suggest consideration be given to raising the target to 2 million tonnes by the mid-1980s. Lastly, we call on food-aid donors and recipients to have regard to the past deficiencies of some uses of food-aid, and to correct them in the light of other, positive experiences.

Institutions

The Cancun Summit reached considerable agreement on measures in food and agriculture, covering most of the topics we have addressed here. It made one additional recommendation calling for a review of agricultural and food agencies working within the framework of the United Nations. While we are aware of excellent work being done by sections of several institutions, there has been criticism of other activities, of overlapping functions and inadequate coordination. *We support an urgent review of this kind.*

To conclude – as was said in the Report, and as cannot be over-emphasised, the fundamental problem of hunger lies far more with demand than with supply, and as much with national as international action. Thus everything we have said about national and international measures to promote growth, employment and more equal distribution of incomes in developing countries remains important for eradicating hunger: measures in finance, trade and energy no less than in food itself, and all the obligations of developing countries to pursue in their own societies the justice and equality they seek from a new international order. An end to hunger may be a long way off. But determined efforts can be made to move towards it.

Energy

Over the past three years, there has developed widespread complacency about the future stability of energy supplies and prices. This complacency cannot be justified.

It is true that oil prices have substantially softened since their second explosion in 1979, that a great deal more spare capacity for producing oil now exists in the world and that the consumption of energy in the North has become considerably more efficient. While real GDP in the OECD countries was 19 per cent higher in 1980 than in 1973, energy consumption was only 4 per cent higher and oil consumption was actually 3 per cent lower.

However, five factors argue against complacency by the consumers. First, a large proportion of the reduced consumption of oil is a result of the recession, and may therefore be reversed as soon as world economic growth revives. Second, in most developing countries, more efficient use of energy in production is usually impossible because at their stage of development economic growth typically requires more energy per unit of output; and many of them have in any case achieved such increases in efficiency as are possible. Third, given that political instability or regional tensions helped bring about both the major increases in the price of oil in the 1970s, one cannot be sure that they will not do so again. Fourth, since the price of oil is denominated in US dollars, the recent dramatic appreciation of the dollar has meant that for many countries, both developed and developing, the real price of oil has dropped only marginally in real terms, if at all. Finally, these fluctuations in the price of oil give rise to changes in the terms of trade, the ability to service debt and the distribution among countries of global payments deficits and surpluses. This in turn creates instability in world trade and financial markets. The interconnections between energy, trade, indebtedness and the financial markets are therefore numerous.

Supply gaps still a threat

The need for consumers to avoid undue complacency about the future of oil is confirmed by the overwhelming majority of forecasts.[41] These foresee a potential supply deficiency in the late 1980s of millions of barrels of oil per day, possibly reaching, according to the International Energy Agency's (IEA) latest *World Energy Outlook*, between 9–21 million barrels per day by the end of the century. Energy needs will not be fully met from sources other than oil. Thus the fairly modest expected growth rates in energy demand will not be satisfied unless oil production can rise more than seems likely. The scenario for an oil price explosion resides in that simple inequality.

The overall health of the international economy clearly requires a stable price for oil. Sudden increases in oil prices seriously exacerbate indebtedness and reduce growth in scores of countries in both North and South. When the oil price goes down, the ability of oil exporters to import, to service debt and to provide employment for workers from other countries is diminished, which damages exports, other foreign exchange earnings and jobs in the consuming countries. The latter are driven to more aggressive export policies in order to earn foreign exchange to pay for crucial imports, as has occurred in a number of East Asian countries, exacerbating protectionist pressures in the North. Bilateral trade arrangements, often infringing the rules of international trade, also proliferate as countries seek to make bargains with oil producers to secure their supplies.

International arrangements

Given the continued potential for instability in the world oil market, and the need for more stable prices, it remains desirable to pursue an agreement between consumers and producers of oil, as we proposed in our Report, which would include assurances on the future of supplies and prices, including security of supplies for the poorest countries. In return for such assurances, the major consumers would need to offer the producers a means of guaranteeing the value of their surplus revenues. And they must be prepared to negotiate such a 'deal' in the context of a wider package of policies which will assist the development of the South as a whole. The OPEC countries have repeatedly made it clear that they will not be prepared to strike a deal confined to energy, but would want to relate it to wider North–South issues, possibly also to a Middle East political statement. The oil price is one of the South's (and the Middle Eastern countries') few potentially powerful levers for change; they will only agree to an arrangement which offers them substantial benefits.

Even if the political conditions for reaching conclusions do not exist at present, *we believe Northern countries should begin a dialogue with OPEC countries over possible future collaboration on energy.* It was shortsighted of the IEA in its otherwise excellent *World Energy Outlook* not even to refer to the possibility of such international cooperation. It speaks of market forces and supplements to them, of encouraging efficiency gains and alternative energy sources; but it ignores the need for discussions between the main consumers and producers of oil. We believe these discussions should also involve Eastern Europe, with whom the West's energy interdependence is growing – a fact which is itself a potential cause of international tension.

The 1981 UN Conference on Energy
A UN Conference on New and Renewable Sources of Energy (NRSE) took place in Nairobi in August 1981. It was able to agree on a programme of action, but not on the funds or institutional mechanisms to carry it forward. The Programme's objectives are to promote NRSE by (a) strengthening international cooperation for research and development and the transfer of relevant technology, (b) mobilising resources for the process, (c) providing for

exchange of information and manpower training to accelerate the use of NRSE in developing countries and (d) promoting and supporting national energy programmes.

At a follow-up meeting in Rome in June 1982 little progress was made. On institutional matters, the developing countries in the Group of 77 wanted a new intergovernmental group within the UN, which was resisted by both the USA and the USSR. On funding, while there was agreement that additional resources were needed, there was none on where they should come from or how they would be channelled: industrial countries (again excluding the USA and USSR) favoured the idea of establishing a new energy agency, possibly affiliated to the World Bank, for investment to develop the Third World's energy resources.

Promoting energy research and production in the Third World
Left to itself, private enterprise often does not undertake sufficient exploration for, and production of, energy in the Third World. The absence of quick profits, uncertainties about the political futures of the host countries or fears about the reliability of contracts with governments may all deter companies from making potentially profitable investments in exploration and production, or in tailoring their research and development programmes to the needs of developing countries.

In our Report we called for increased investment in developing countries' energy resources and for the promotion and dissemination of research and its results. For the latter purpose, we recommended that a global energy research centre should be created under UN auspices to coordinate information and projections and to support research on new energy resources. There are also further specific needs: to assist developing countries in negotiating energy contracts and assuring energy supplies; to assist them in the more appropriate use of traditional energy sources, particularly fuel-wood, which is now being

136

used at an unsustainable rate with profoundly damaging effects on the environment and agriculture of the world; to examine the feasibility of alternative traditional energy sources, particularly cost-effective and low-technology means of generating energy; and to promote sub-regional and regional cooperation in reducing energy costs and assuring energy supplies for developing countries.

We believe that these tasks could be undertaken by the proposed 'energy affiliate' of the World Bank which has entered international discussion in the last two years. The advantage of pursuing them within the Bank would be to take advantage both of its considerable expertise and of its high credibility in the eyes of investors and financial markets. At the same time, its separation from the existing structure of the World Bank would enable it to have a form of management and decision-making that reserved less power for the industrialised countries and therefore enabled more power to be given to those developing countries, such as the major oil producers, which are in a position to contribute to financing the new affiliate. In Chapter 2, we proposed the establishment of a separate capital account with a higher gearing ratio in the World Bank which might be used for the affiliate. We also referred to the importance which a voting structure more favourable to developing countries could have on their willingness to contribute additional finance to the international financial institutions.

It may or may not prove possible to incorporate the research and other specific functions we have just described in a new agency whose primary function is investment and exploration. If it does not, or if such an agency does not come into being, we would continue to press for an international research centre such as we proposed in our Report.

The creation of an energy affiliate was discussed at the Cancun Summit, and was agreed to be necessary by almost all those present. However, the current United States Administration has consistently opposed its creation. The reasons for that opposition have not been fully disclosed. There have been hostile representations from some US oil companies. We believe they are mistaken. Much of what an energy agency would do – exploration, pre-investment, technical cooperation – would be positively beneficial to private companies wishing to invest in this sector. And as World Bank publications have themselves observed,[42] some of the investments which would be valuable to the countries concerned are not of much interest to foreign companies, especially the development of small hydrocarbon deposits; while others are beyond their scope, such as major hydro-electric schemes. Studies have shown large benefits to the US from investments in Third World energy. The opposition of the US Administration thus appears to us baffling.

The creation of an energy agency of this kind is too urgent a task to allow any one country to prevent it being set up. If the US is unwilling to participate, other countries, particularly from Europe, Australasia, Japan and OPEC, should agree to go ahead without Washington. Legally, there is no reason why this should not be done, leaving it open for the US to join at a later date.

However, if these countries do not wish to create a precedent of taking initiatives within the World Bank without the participation of the US, they should set up an energy agency which is separate from that institution.

We could not view the absence of the US from this vital initiative with equanimity. We therefore appeal to the US administration to reconsider its position, in its own interest and that of the international community.

5   The Negotiating Process

The North–South dialogue can neither be divorced from the world economic crisis nor be deferred for attention until after the crisis is resolved and recovery is on the way. In our Report we made proposals for injecting new purpose into the dialogue. This has acquired a new urgency. The desperate situation facing the poorer developing countries and recent dramatic demonstrations of interdependence between North and South in such areas as trade and finance make that clear. But the global economic recession and stalemate in the North–South dialogue have been mutually reinforcing, and the dialogue has become quiescent and unproductive. How can the vicious circle be broken?

Improving the process
For progress to be made on the substantive recommendations in our Report and in this document, it must be recognised that the negotiating process itself has created obstacles to agreement. In our 'overview' observations on International Organisations and Negotiations in Chapter 16 of our Report, we drew attention to the need for the United Nations system to be strengthened and made more efficient. We put forward there a number of recommendations to that end, including the need for greater coordination between UN agencies and programmes, and diminished bureaucratisation. We reiterate those recommendations now. But we go further;

particularly in the context of the urgent need for better results from the negotiating process.

New and better ways must be found of developing the convergences of view which could help to resolve the current crisis. All parties can contribute to breaking out of a stereotyped negotiating process which has failed to serve the cause either of enlarging understanding or of promoting consensus. To date, with only a few exceptions, the process has tended to polarise positions and diminish hope of agreement. Much has been wrong with the nature of the dialogue.

Fortunately, there is increasing recognition on all sides that obstacles to progress arise not only from issues of substance but also from attitudes, procedures and institutional considerations. These questions have recently received serious examination by a high level Commonwealth Group of Experts comprising people with considerable practical experience in the North–South negotiating process. Their report, *The North–South Dialogue: Making it Work*, supports most of the approaches in our own Report. In their more comprehensive treatment of the subject, however, they have developed a number of detailed proposals. They have produced a frank assessment of the defects in existing approaches and attitudes of both the North and the South, and have recommended new, realistic approaches to the evolution of a more constructive and workable dialogue. Their report deserves serious and urgent attention by the international community. We draw attention here to some of the more important areas in which progress is needed.

Attitudes of the North
Basic attitudes on the part of the North are obviously a critical factor. The industrialised countries have important long-term interests in the evolution of a cooperative and stable international system. It would therefore be wise for them to accept the reality of the Third World as a continuing and significant political grouping, and work

140

towards improving the effectiveness of multilateral and group diplomacy. Further, the greatly increased interdependence of the world economy requires coordinated international action. Positive, flexible and timely policies are more effective in dealing with genuine and powerful agencies of change in international relations than are negative reactions and passive resistance. The North therefore should respond positively to sound proposals by the South, and also put forward proposals of its own. This would make for greater pragmatism and realism. The countries of the North should fully recognise the whole complex of their political, strategic and economic interests in global negotiations. This implies their accepting the need for power-sharing in international economic decision-making. They should also more readily accept, as they already do at home, the need in some circumstances to modify the operation of market forces in the international sphere.

Eastern Europe and China

In recent years the Soviet Union, other East European countries and China have become increasingly integrated into the world economy. China, Hungary and Romania are now members of the Bretton Woods institutions. Their increasing involvement in international capital markets and in trade in agriculture, energy and technology has given them a very much greater stake in international economic cooperation. We welcome the increasing participation of China in the North–South dialogue; but we regret the decision of most East European countries to stand aside from it. The dialogue is now about what should be done in the future – a future in which they share – and we call on them to play a part in it commensurate with their economic weight and political importance.

The South

On the part of the South, there must be greater recognition that while the North too has a major interest in improved policies, the South's interest is more direct and urgent; being the side more convinced of the need for change, it must be prepared to take the initiative to secure a more productive dialogue. The South would be more successul if it adopted a more persuasive negotiating style, devoted greater attention to mutual interests in submitting proposals, and showed less rigidity in the forms and procedures of its group system, and a greater readiness to use more specialised fora and non-global approaches. The South should be more hesitant to resort to voted resolutions and majority decisions. It must be prepared to make greater financial contributions in support of proposals which require capital subscriptions. And it must acknowledge that its economic progress depends at least as much on the adoption and implementation of sound economic policies as it does on international action.

A new start

The North–South dialogue, to date forcefully and often creatively pursued by the South, has had an inhibiting effect on the North, which has turned to mainly defensive postures and negative attitudes. It matters less where the balance of blame lies than that all sides need to place the dialogue on a new basis – one in which North and South freely accept the need to search together for solutions that are palpably in the interest of both and engage creatively in it. There is no time to lose in making a new start. If the style and tactics of strident demand and mute response continue, both development and world recovery will be victims; people in both the South and the North will face mounting hardship.

But attitudinal changes though important will not be sufficient. Procedural and institutional changes will also be required. There must be recognition that not all issues have the same interest for all countries and regions. Indeed, some issues do not have a North–South dimension alone. There should therefore be willingness to accept diversity in the negotiating process. A serious impediment to progress has been the need to obtain consensus in the whole global community before decisions are taken. There should be a greater readiness to proceed with changes, even without the agreement of some countries, by those who are prepared to take the necessary action. The latter will of course only be willing to do so if it does not imply shouldering unfair burdens.

Greater use should be made of single-issue negotiating conferences, since they are often more efficient in reaching agreement; witness the UNCTAD Conference on the Least Developed Countries. In doing so, however, one should not lose sight of the ways in which different issues are naturally interrelated, or of negotiations in fora which deal with wider sets of issues. Single-issue negotiations are complementary to and supportive of universal negotiations, and not contradictory to them. Indeed, the former have usually arisen out of the latter.

Much greater use should also be made of the small-group negotiating technique – used to good effect in the Law of the Sea Conference. Despite the participation of 153 countries in the Conference as a whole, the key draft agreements were worked out by a forum of only 21 countries, which in its turn spawned smaller and even more informal groups of delegates as and when necessary. This remarkable procedure neither required the abandonment of the old groups (B, D, and 77 in the UN's nomenclature), nor did it undermine their integrity in other fora. Indeed, universal fora and negotiations in small groups are mutually supportive, rather than in any way antithetical. The fact that the code on the Law of the Sea later had to be renegotiated in no way reflects on the validity of the procedure by which agreement was reached.

Unfortunately, many attempts in the past to use small groups have been frustrated by the failure to insist on their being kept limited. They have been constituted as small groups, but other countries have tended to tag on in an unplanned way. The time has surely come to make a determined attempt to sustain negotiations in small, closed and broadly representative groups rather than open-ended ones – provided final agreement is left to plenaries where the principle of universality could be reasserted. We emphasise representativeness since, in the GATT, preliminary negotiations tend to take place bilaterally or in small groups which, being constituted informally, tend as a result to involve the major trading partners and to produce final decisions which mainly reflect the interests of these countries. *Efforts should also be made to secure higher levels of representation at negotiating conferences and greater use of ministerial representation*, which has also in the past tended to produce better results, as in the UNCTAD Conference on Debt Relief.

Public opinion, development education and coordination
In our Report we stressed the importance of support by Governments for development education. This is important to ease the constraint on long-term action imposed by electoral processes. If societies do not educate their citizens for the interdependent world they have inherited, their governments will find it difficult to take the decisions that an interdependent world economy demands. We therefore re-emphasise the importance we attach to this. Another crucial requirement is for greater coordination of development policies within national administrations in developed countries. Both purposes – development education and coordination – could be served by the establishment in developed countries of Ministries or Departments concerned with development cooperation – and not merely with aid programmes. We urge their establishment where they do not yet exist.

Research on international development issues
The negotiating process could be assisted by increased research on international economic issues. Recognition of this inadequacy has led to a recent proposal by the UN University to establish under its auspices a World Institute

for Development Economics Research. *We welcome this proposal and commend it for international support.* We believe it would usefully supplement research being undertaken by existing institutions and the independent and international character of the proposed Institute would give research a global perspective which growing interdependence is making increasingly necessary.

A Third World secretariat

It is also urgent to improve coordination between countries of the South. The North already has, through OECD and other organisations, the machinery of coordination for its international negotiating stance. But developing countries do not have adequate support in technical and analytical work or statistical services, and have real difficulties in developing and supporting negotiating proposals suitable to their diverse interests and policy objectives. During negotiations they are also hampered by the lack of readily available expert back-up. That compounds the difficulties caused by the nature of their representation at negotiations: many developing countries cannot send specialists to meetings, but rely on foreign ministry officers whose skills are political and administrative rather than technical. The formation and renegotiation of positions is further hindered by the lack of fast-moving communication between officials abroad and their capitals. And the absence of technical support from an organisation of their own causes pressures by developing countries on officials of international organisations to play a partisan role, which is undesirable in itself.

We are firmly of the opinion that many of the Group of 77's negotiating difficulties could be avoided if there were an arrangement to give them technical support. In our Report we advocated the establishment of a Third World secretariat. While some members of the Group of 77 have been sceptical, others have seen its virtues. Such a body would comprise a group of technical experts whose competence extended over the range of North–South

145

issues. They would liaise with other institutions, avoiding duplication of work. *We strongly urge the establishment of such a technical support group.*

South–South cooperation

A Third World secretariat would also provide technical support for cooperation between developing countries in the areas of finance, trade, food and energy. This would be a complement rather than an alternative to North–South cooperation in these areas. Economic development must be enhanced by the exploitation of all opportunities to promote progress. Moreover, as we indicated above, where developing countries show greater readiness to provide financial support for their proposals or take practical initiatives on their own, they are likely to induce greater progress in negotiations with the North. Finance and trade offer particular scope for South–South cooperation and it is likely that the establishment of Southern financial institutions will encourage the North to agree to the further development of the World Bank and the IMF along the lines we have suggested.

Reform of institutions

The inadequate degree of power possessed by developing countries in international financial institutions is a major obstacle to North–South cooperation. It generates institutional proliferation as developing countries seek to create new institutions in the running of which they have a greater say. And it leads to often prolonged arguments between developed and developing countries over which institutions should undertake negotiations on particular issues, based on the extent of control which each group of countries exercises in them. This has happened during the attempt to launch a new round of Global Negotiations. Several Northern countries have been adamant that the competence of the Bretton Woods agencies should in no way be diluted by any form of negotiation on financial issues at the UN.

146

In reality no resolution in the UN would be binding on the agencies in question. But greater understanding is needed on both sides – from the North, that the power structure of these organisations still largely reflects the distribution of financial and economic power of thirty-five years ago, and is ripe for change; and from the South, that they must give due weight to perceptions of prudence and good management of those developed countries whose continued financial support for the institutions is so necessary for the maintenance and expansion of their operations. Greater progress on power-sharing within the Bretton Woods institutions, a greater separation between voting power and eligibility for financial support in the IMF and improved negotiating processes at the GATT to encourage greater involvement of the developing countries and the smaller developed countries would undoubtedly reduce the procedural wrangles which beset international negotiations. As the recent experience of the GATT Ministerial Meeting underlines, developed-country dominance within international institutions does not ensure that they are effective nor that their deliberations are productive – even in terms of the principles and objectives they were established to serve.

Towards the Global Round

Changes in the negotiating process will take time before they can be fully implemented. But even the beginning of reform would facilitate progress, and such progress would in turn help in the process of confidence-building which is so greatly needed for the changes envisaged in the North–South dialogue.

Forthcoming meetings offer an opportunity to begin the process of confidence-building. Significant decisions on issues bearing on the present crisis could help to set the new path. A start could be made by agreement to launch the Global Round of Negotiations which has now become the symbol of progress in the North–South dialogue. As did the Commonwealth Expert Group in its report, we believe that the UN General Assembly, being the most representative body in the international system, should play a central role in global negotiations and that this need not be inconsistent with respect for the role and competence of the specialised agencies. We endorse the view of the Group however that in order to ensure this:

the General Assembly will have to equip itself in two ways. First, it will have to constitute a small, representative and efficient negotiating and overviewing body. Second, it will have to attract the attendance of representatives of high political stature and professional competence so that it will be able to carry out the central role and overview function which are envisaged.

UNCTAD VI

The major North–South Conference ahead is UNCTAD VI. It will consider the world economic situation, with special emphasis on development and protectionism and structural adjustment. In the preparations for the Conference progress has been made in providing for more streamlined discussions than in past UNCTAD sessions, and on the whole there is a mood of recognition of the seriousness of the problems faced by the world economy and of greater realism in expectations.

It is extremely important that there should be a positive response to these signals and the opportunity be taken to arrive at decisions that would ease the plight of developing countries and make some contribution to world economic recovery. We would encourage the Conference to concentrate on issues relevant to the current crisis, where both sides have an interest in reaching agreement and where outstanding questions have now become urgent. The disappointing outcome of the GATT Ministerial Meeting and the dangers to the financial system point to the need for effective decisions to be taken swiftly.

To maximise the opportunities offered by the timely occasion of UNCTAD VI, a process of political dialogue is needed at a high level, that anticipates its potential and makes a determined, perhaps innovative, effort to secure optimal returns for both development and world economic recovery. We feel that even a few world leaders mindful of the opportunities and ready to seize them can greatly enlarge the possibilities of success at Belgrade, by helping it to set a new and more promising style in world economic consultation. We encourage all such initiatives. Indeed, we go further and urge political leaders to respond to the challenge for effective political consultation on the issues we have raised in this Memorandum, by exploring in new, perhaps informal, ways all opportunities for bridging differences of perception, of understanding, and of approaches to solutions, that now unnecessarily divide them and their peoples. Much can be achieved by the bold initiatives of the few.

Ways forward: like-minded countries

In the past, progress in the dialogue has been hampered by the need to obtain global consensus. Backsliding by a few countries or the dilution of resolutions to secure consensus have not been conducive to progress. The emergence of an informal grouping of like-minded countries in the North which are more sympathetic to the development needs of the South has been a significant development. It has already contributed to progress in some of the negotiations by the collective pressure it has been able to exert in favour of more favourable development policies. In the light of the continuing slow progress in the dialogue the time has come for the like-minded countries to move beyond an informal 'pressure group' role. They would make a greater contribution to progress by more formal and independent action in supporting a more active role by the North and also in negotiating arrangements directly with groups of developing countries where this is feasible. In this connection *discussions between like-minded countries of the North and groups of interested countries in the South could be very helpful in pushing the dialogue forward and we strongly support moves which have already been made in this direction.* However, we fully recognise that small

149

groups should not attempt to bind those who do not participate in them.

A second North–South Summit

In the light of the deepening of the world economic crisis, concerted and determined action is needed to secure early progress on the emergency measures required. *We believe that there remains a strong case for a second 'Cancun' Summit*, which we hope would lead to further summits if the participants feel such a process to be of continuing value. The worldwide dimensions of the current crisis and its persistence justify another attempt at holding a summit. A second summit would benefit greatly from the experience of the first. An essential requirement would be adequate preparation, including a measure of pre-negotiation between high-level representatives of the heads of state or government.

Finally, while it is always preferable to have a representative summit, if the process of arranging such a meeting is being frustrated by the reluctance or negative postures of one or two major countries, serious consideration should be given to proceeding without them. In fact, consideration might also be given to summits involving countries where the possibilities of convergence are greater, for example the like-minded countries of the North and countries of the South. Agreements between a limited group of countries could then, hopefully, be broadened to include others not present. If we are to make the North– South dialogue work it must, at the very least, derive an impetus towards success from political decision-makers themselves. Without that impetus the dialogue will remain a wasteland of frustrated effort and defeated hope.

Conclusions

We therefore propose:

● More positive and realistic attitudes to negotiations on the part of both North and South.

- Resort to summitry to give political impetus to negotiations, with adequate preparation and pre-negotiation.
- An early launching of the Global Round of Negotiations on international economic cooperation for development, with the UN General Assembly playing a central role, assisted by a small, representative and efficient negotiating and overviewing body, with representation at a high level of political stature and professional competence.
- A bold attempt by the 'like-minded' countries to forge ahead in North–South negotiations.
- More use of single-issue conferences as a complement to universal negotiations; more negotiations conducted in representative small groups; and more flexible use of the group system.
- Willingness to accept diversity in the negotiating process in terms of groupings between which negotiations take place; and readiness on occasion to proceed with detailed negotiations and even implementation without global consensus by excluding reluctant or uncooperative countries.
- A Third World secretariat to provide technical support to developing countries in preparing negotiating positions and conducting negotiations.
- Greater South–South cooperation and readiness on the part of the South to subscribe capital to back its proposals.
- Improved coordination of national policies on North–South issues, between departments of government and representatives at negotiations and their governments, and between international organisations.
- More adequate support for development education in the North, from public and private sources, to bring development issues more firmly into the consciousness of public opinion.
- Continued efforts to rationalise the workings of the institutions within the UN system.

Resumé of Principal Proposals

Below we summarise our main proposals on finance, trade, food, energy and the negotiating process. We are fully aware that these must be complemented by coordination for expansion on the part of the North and policies for greater effectiveness of economic management in the South.

Finance

To assist resolution of the current balance of payments, debt and banking crisis, and to help promote recovery in developing and industrial countries, we propose for immediate action:

The IMF

- A substantial new SDR allocation with particular attention to the needs of developing countries.
- At least a doubling of IMF quotas.
- An emergency borrowing authority to support developing countries through enlargement and reform of the General Arrangements to Borrow.
- Increased borrowing from central banks; and borrowing from capital markets.
- Enlargement and improvement of the Compensatory Financing Facility.

Changes in conditionality as follows:

- The IMF's conditionality to be made more appropriate to the situation of the borrower, especially with respect to countries' capabilities to borrow in commercial markets, their needs for balance of payments support from official agencies, and their abilities to correct payments deficits over given time periods. In particular low-income countries with limited access to market borrowing, heavy dependence on official agencies for balance of payments support, and restricted capacity for rapid economic transformation, should have far greater availability of low-conditionality finance when temporary deficits arise due to circumstances beyond their control.

- Countries to be encouraged by the enlarged availability of low-conditionality credits to come to the IMF at an early stage of anticipated difficulties.

- Greater attention to be paid to supply relative to demand conditions, so that payments deficits are corrected by an appropriate mix of policies with less exclusive concentration on demand constraints, devaluation and credit ceilings as the main instruments of adjustment.

- The IMF in framing its programmes to give greater weight to output, growth, employment and income-distribution considerations, relative to its past emphasis on the control of inflation and payments deficits, and to obey more fully its own new guidelines of 1979 which call for paying due regard to the domestic, social and political objectives of member countries.

- Improvement in terms and conditions for poorer borrowers financed by augmenting the subsidy account with the proceeds of controlled sales of IMF gold, voluntary transfers of SDRs from developed countries, contributions from members, repayments from the Trust Fund, or savings from charging market interest rates on credits to better-off borrowers.

The World Bank and International Development Association

● An increase in programme lending by changing the 10-per-cent limit on such lending as a proportion of total lending to 30 per cent.
● A strong commitment to a real increase in funds for the seventh IDA replenishment, to raise aid levels for low-income countries.
● Augmented borrowing authority for the World Bank, by a combination of an increase in the gearing ratio, on a step-by-step basis if necessary, to double the present ratio, and increased capital subscriptions.

Other aspects of aid

● Aid to the poorest countries to be doubled in real terms by 1985, through bilateral and multilateral channels, and the target of 0.15 per cent of GNP for such aid to be met by the donors.
● Full implementation of the agreement to waive official debt for the least developed countries.
● A new commitment to reach the 0.7 per cent of GNP target for Official Development Assistance within five years.
● Greatly increased bilateral aid for programme lending and local and recurrent costs.
● Greater urgency in measures for enhancing aid effectiveness, including aid coordination.
● Greater national and international support for the work of voluntary agencies, on a matching basis with their own subscribed funds.

Debt negotiations

● Strengthening informal coordination among the IMF, the World Bank, other official lenders and the commercial banks, to ensure adequate provision of resources through the support of all lenders.

Bank for International Settlements
- Bridge-finance operations by the BIS to be expanded and developed countries to encourage their central banks to provide short-term deposits to it for that purpose.

Private capital
The above measures would create a framework of confidence in which private bank lending to developing countries would be able to expand. Further measures to support private capital and private foreign investment are also proposed:

- Consideration of a multilateral investment insurance mechanism along the lines of that currently under examination by the World Bank.
- Additional support for the World Bank's International Finance Corporation.
- Consideration of an Investment Credit Guarantee Fund to promote project lending by commercial banks.

The expansion of foreign equity investment in developing countries we call for requires, in addition to the above measures, the establishment of a better framework for investments. We therefore propose:

- Renewed efforts to negotiate a framework for international investment satisfactory to investors and home and host countries.

Financial cooperation among developing countries
Increased cooperation within the South by:

- Strengthening regional payments arrangements.
- Expansion of developing countries' financial facilities, including considering the establishment of a Third-World Bank.

- Support for enlarging, refinancing and guaranteeing developing countries' export credit facilities.
- Increased direct investment in the Third World by developing countries.

The above proposals are all relevant to the current situation, partly to avoid a worsening trend and possible financial collapse. But additional measures are also needed. We propose *for further action*:

- Reform of the IMF and World Bank in the direction of greater power-sharing.
- International monetary reform, centred on the SDR as the principal reserve asset, the substitution account, modalities of intervention to create greater stability in exchange rates, a new definition of the obligations of surplus countries to share in global adjustments, and a more strongly counter-cyclical role for the IMF.
- An authoritative international review of the future of the Bretton Woods institutions, to lead to a world conference on international financial institutions.
- Provision for long-term funding of developing countries' debt.
- Continued consideration of a World Development Fund within the context of Global Negotiations in the United Nations.
- Measures for international revenue generation.

Trade

We propose the following emergency measures which need to be taken urgently to improve the world trading environment:

- A reinforcement of the commitment to the principles of an open, rule-governed trading system and of the undertaking to resist protectionist pressures in formulating and implementing national trade policies and laws.

- A new safeguard mechanism clearly defining the circumstances in which protective action under Article XIX of the GATT is justified, and the scope and duration – which should be limited – of such action.
- Early elimination of all remaining barriers in developed countries on the import of tropical products.
- Early ratification of the Common Fund, and agreement on new international commodity arrangements and on enlarging compensation for developing countries' periodic losses of commodity export earnings.

In addition it is necessary to make an early start towards seeking longer-term solutions to several other problems in international trade. With that objective in mind, we make the following proposals among others:

- Further strengthening of procedures and powers to provide an effective mechanism for settling international trade disputes.
- Implementation of measures to improve market access for processed commodities, particularly in the developed countries, by the elimination of tariff escalation and non-tariff barriers.
- Closer consultation between GATT, UNCTAD and other international bodies under which not only trade issues but also structural adjustment and other relevant national policies can be discussed and analysed, with a view to obtaining more fruitful international negotiations.

Food

Measures to raise food and agricultural production in developing countries, especially the poorest, and improve food security, by:

- Preparation of national food strategies by developing countries, to be supported as necessary by increased and improved aid.

- Support for increased international food reserves, including meeting the agreed target of 500,000 tonnes annually for the Emergency Food Reserve and preparing for its future enlargement, and assistance for developing a programme of country-owned reserves.
- Regional programmes to combat ecological deterioration and improve resource use.
- Greatly increased support for agricultural research, especially to develop improved crop varieties and methods of cultivation for Africa, and the development of indigenous research capacity.
- Increased food-aid, under continuous surveillance to eliminate possible harmful effects, and an increase in the target for minimum quantities of food aid to 10 million tonnes.

Energy

We propose:

- A new energy agency to increase energy production in developing countries, preferably affiliated to the World Bank, with full international participation.
- Institutional support for energy research and the dissemination of its results, within the new energy agency if it is set up, or within a separate agency.
- A dialogue between major oil-consuming and oil-producing countries to consider arrangements beneficial to all parties, including safeguarding supplies to the poorest countries, and long-term stability in oil markets.

The Negotiating Process

The negotiating process has been an obstacle to progress on North–South issues and should be improved by:

- Urgent world economic consultations on the adoption and implementation of emergency measures for recovery and development, bearing in mind the opportunities offered by the Sixth Session of UNCTAD which is to take place in Yugoslavia in June 1983.

- More positive and realistic attitudes to negotiations on the part of both North and South.
- Resort to the Summit process to give political impetus to negotiations, with adequate preparation and pre-negotiation.
- An early launching of the Global Round of Negotiations on international economic cooperation for development, with the UN General Assembly playing a central role, assisted by a small representative and efficient negotiating and overviewing body, with representation at a high level of political stature and professional competence.
- More use of single-issue conferences; more negotiations conducted in representative small groups; and more flexible use of the group system.
- Willingness to accept diversity in the negotiating process in terms of groupings between which negotiations take place; and readiness on occasion to proceed with detailed negotiations and even implementation without global consensus by excluding reluctant or uncooperative countries.
- A Third World secretariat to provide technical support to developing countries in preparing negotiating positions and conducting negotiations.
- Greater South–South cooperation and readiness on the part of the South to subscribe capital to back its proposals.
- More adequate support for development education in the North, from public and private sources, to bring development issues more firmly into the consciousness of public opinion.

Annexe

The Commission and Its Work

The Independent Commission on International Development Issues was launched at Gymnich, Germany, on 9 December 1977. At its opening meeting, the Commission agreed on its terms of reference and a working agenda.

The suggestion of creating such a Commission under the chairmanship of Willy Brandt had first been advanced by Robert S. McNamara, then President of the World Bank, in a speech in Boston on 15 January 1977. McNamara again proposed the idea during his address to the Annual Meeting of the IMF and World Bank in Washington in the autumn of that year.

The Commission was to be independent. Members were invited by the Chairman to serve in a private capacity, not under governmental instructions. He was anxious that Third World members should not be in a minority position.

The Commissioners

Chairman
Willy Brandt   Bonn, Federal Republic of Germany. Chairman of the Social Democratic Party, Federal Chancellor 1969–74, Minister of Foreign Affairs 1966–9, Mayor of Berlin 1957–66, Nobel Peace Prize 1971.

Members
Abdlatif Y. Al-Hamad   Kuwait. Minister of Finance, Member of Governing Body, Institute of Development Studies, Sussex, Member of Visiting Committee, Center for Middle East Studies, Harvard University, Director-General of Kuwait Fund for Arabic Economic Development, Trustee, Kuwait Institute of Economic and Social Planning in the Middle East.

160

Rodrigo Botero Montoya   Bogotá, Colombia. Economist, Editor and Publisher of *Estrategia Economica y Financiera*, Minister of Finance 1974–6, Executive Director, Foundation for Higher Education and Development (FEDESARROLLO) 1970–4, Special Presidential Assistant for Economic Affairs in Bogotá 1966–70.

Antoine Kipsa Dakouré   Ouagadougou, Upper Volta. Ambassador to the EEC, Adviser to the President of Upper Volta 1976–80, Coordinating Minister for Drought Control in the Sahel 1973–5, Minister of Planning 1970–6, Minister of Agriculture 1966–70.

Eduardo Frei Montalva   Santiago, Chile. 1911–82.

Katharine Graham   Washington, DC, USA. Chairman of the Board, Washington Post Co. since 1963.

Edward Heath   London, United Kingdom. Politician, MP, Prime Minister 1970–4, Leader of the Conservative Party 1965–75, Secretary of State for Industry, Trade and Regional Development 1963–4, Leader of the British Delegation to UNCTAD 1964, Lord Privy Seal at the Foreign Office 1960–3, Minister of Labour 1959–60.

Amir H. Jamal   Dar-es-Salaam, Tanzania. Minister of Finance, Minister of Communications and Transport 1977–9, Minister of Finance and Economic Planning 1975–7, Minister for Commerce and Industries 1972–5, Minister of Finance 1965–72, Minister of Economic Planning 1964–5, Minister of Communications and Power 1962–4.

Lakshmi Kant Jha   New Delhi, India. Chairman, Economic Administration Reforms Commission, Governor of Jammu and Kashmir 1977–81, Chairman of UN Group of Eminent Persons on Multilateral Corporations 1973–5, Ambassador to the USA 1970–3, Governor of the Reserve Bank of India 1967–70.

Khatijah Ahmad   Kuala Lumpur, Malaysia. Economist and banker, Managing Director of KAF Discounts Ltd since 1974, Director of Administration and Secretary of National Paddy and Rice Authority 1971–3.

Adam Malik   Jakarta, Indonesia. Vice-President, President of National Assembly 1971–2, Minister of Commerce 1963–5, Ambassador to the USSR 1959–63.

Haruki Mori   Tokyo, Japan. Ambassador to the United Kingdom 1972–5, Vice Minister in the Ministry of Foreign Affairs 1970–2, Ambassador to the OECD 1964–7.

Joe Morris   Victoria, Canada. President-Emeritus of Canadian Labour Congress and Vice-Chairman of International Labour Organisation's Governing Body 1970–9, Chairman, ILO Governing Body 1977–8, Vice-President ICFTU 1976–8.

Olof Palme   Stockholm, Sweden. Prime Minister, Chairman of the Social Democratic Party, Prime Minister 1969–76, Minister of Education and Culture 1967–9, Minister of Communications 1965–7, Minister without Portfolio 1963–5.

Peter G. Peterson*   New York, USA. Chairman of the Board of Lehman Bros. Kuhn Loeb, Secretary of Commerce 1972–3, Assistant to the President of USA for International Economic Affairs and Executive Director of the Council on International Economic Policy 1971–2.
    *Mr Peterson did not participate in the preparation of the Memorandum.

Edgard Pisani*   Paris, France. Member of the Commission of the European Communities, Senator 1974–81, Member of European Parliament, Minister of National Equipment 1966–7, Minister of Agriculture 1961–6.
    *Mr Pisani replaced Mr Pierre Mendès-France, former Prime Minister of France, who had originally been a member and participated in the Commission's work but had to resign for personal reasons in summer 1978.

Shridath Ramphal   Georgetown, Guyana. Commonwealth Secretary-General, Minister of Foreign Affairs and Justice 1972–5, Attorney-General and Minister of State for External Affairs, 1966–72.

Layachi Yaker   Algiers, Algeria. Ambassador to the United States, Ambassador to the USSR 1979–82, Member of the Central Committee of the Party of the National Liberation Front, Member of Parliament and Vice-President, National People's Assembly 1977–9, Minister of Commerce 1969–77, Minister Plenipotentiary, Director of Economic, Cultural and Social Affairs, Ministry of Foreign Affairs 1962–9.

Ex-officio Members

Jan P. Pronk   The Hague, Netherlands. Deputy Secretary General of UNCTAD, Member of Parliament 1971–3 and since 1978, Minister for Development Cooperation 1973–7, Research Assistant to Professor Jan Tinbergen 1965–71, Honorary Treasurer, ICIDI.

Goran Ohlin   Stockholm, Sweden. Professor of Economics at Uppsala University since 1969, Staff Member of the Pearson Commission 1968–9, Fellow of the Development Centre of OECD, Paris 1962–6, Consultant to various international organisations, Executive Secretary, ICIDI 1978–9.

Dragoslav Avramović   Belgrade, Yugoslavia. Special Adviser to UNCTAD Secretary General, Senior economic staff positions in World Bank 1965–77, Director, Economics Department, Industrialisation Studies, Commodity Studies, Debt Studies, Special Adviser to UNCTAD on Commodity Stabilisation 1974–5, before 1953, senior posts Government of Yugoslavia and teaching, University of Belgrade, Director of the Secretariat, ICIDI 1978–9.

Staff and Working Group 1982

Robert H. Cassen is a Professorial Fellow in Economics at the Institute of Development Studies, University of Sussex, England.

Simon May is Foreign Affairs Adviser to the Rt. Hon. Edward Heath and a Research Fellow at the International Institute for Strategic Studies, London.

Bishnodat Persaud is Director of the Economic Affairs Division, Commonwealth Secretariat, London.

Anthony Sampson is the author of *Anatomy of Britain, The Money Lenders, The Arms Bazaar* and a number of other best-selling books.

Christel Siebel-Wolters has served as Administrative Assistant to the Chairman on Commission matters.

Gerhard G. Thiebach has headed the Commission's continuing office in The Hague, and served as Executive Assistant to the Chairman on Commission matters.

After two years and ten meetings in different parts of the world, the Commissioners unanimously adopted a Report, which was published in early 1980, entitled *North–South: A Programme for Survival*. The first copy was presented to the UN Secretary General, Kurt Waldheim.

Upon the completion of its task the Commission ceased to exist as a formal body. Its Secretariat was dissolved, and although there was no formal follow-up, a small office was established to deal with requests, comments, etc. The Dutch Government, which had already financed half of the Commission's original budget, supported the follow-up office (IBIDI Independent Bureau for International Development Issues, PO Box 90733, The Hague, Netherlands).

In addition to the Commission's Report selected papers, which formed part of the background to the Commission's deliberations, were published in IBIDI: *The Brandt Commission Papers: Selected Background Papers Prepared for the Independent Commission on International Development Issues, 1978–1979* (Geneva and The Hague: IBIDI, 1981, $15 US). IBIDI also arranged the translation and publication of the Report in various languages. The Brandt Report, as it became known, is now available in the following languages: English, Arabic, Chinese, Danish, Dutch, French, German, Greek, Indonesian, Italian, Japanese, Korean, Malay, Norwegian, Polish, Portuguese, Romanian, Serbo-Croat, Spanish, Swahili, Swedish.

International organisations have acted on some recommendations and continue to study others. The International Monetary Fund and the World Bank, for example, followed up on some suggestions for changes in their operations and policies.

It must be admitted, however, that the Commission's impact has been slow in general and limited in scope. But the deepening world crisis, which has confirmed many of the Commission's worst fears, is changing the minds of many who initially rejected the Report as too pessimistic in its analysis or too radical in its recommendations.

Meetings

The first meeting of Commissioners after publication of the Report took place in The Hague on 15–18 May 1980, at the invitation of the Dutch Government. It provided an opportunity to assess the first reactions to the Report. A public meeting was attended by about 4,000 people who listened to representatives of attended by about 4,000 people who listened to representatives of various social groups give their reactions and assessments of the Report. In the presence of the Royal family and members of the Dutch Government, there was a clear public demand that Commissioners should continue to work for the implementation of their recommendations.

A second meeting was held in Berlin, 29– 31 May 1981, at the invitation of the German Government and hosted by the German Foundation for International Development (DSE). It was attended by special guests: The President of the UN General Assembly, Mr von Wechmar; FAO Director General, Mr Saoma; and Mr Benjenk, Vice-President for Information of the World Bank. The Commissioners were received by the Governing Mayor of Berlin, Mr Hans-Jochen Vogel, and met also with the German Federal Chancellor, Helmut Schmidt. Among other issues, the Commissioners discussed the forthcoming North–South Summit meeting, which was earlier proposed in their Report, and decided to send a message to the Summit participants.

At the invitation of the Government, a third meeting was held in Kuwait, 7–8 January 1982, attended by special guests: Ambassador Kittani, President of the UN General Assembly; Dr Shihata, Director General of the OPEC Fund; Mr Al-Khaled, Director General of the Kuwait Fund for Arab Economic Development, and Dr Lennkh, Special Adviser to the Austrian Chancellor, Bruno Kreisky. Commissioners were received by the Emir of Kuwait and met with various cabinet members. At this meeting Commissioners discussed the results of the Cancun Summit and the deepening world-wide economic crisis. They decided to prepare a new Memorandum and to issue another call for emergency action. An Editorial Group was set up under the leadership of Mr Heath and Mr Ramphal, in consultation with the Chairman, which began working in London to prepare a draft text for submission to the Ottawa meeting.

A fourth meeting took place in Brussels, 22–24 September. Dr Lubbers from the Netherlands and Mr Thorvald Stoltenberg from Norway participated in the discussions as special guests. The Commissioners were the guests of the Commission of the European Communities, whose draft policy memorandum on Community relations with developing countries they were asked to discuss. They also discussed an issues paper dealing with subjects to be included in their new Memorandum. They were received by the President of the Commission of the European

Communities, Mr Gaston Thorn, and met with members of that Commission.

On 11–14 December 1982, a fifth meeting was held in Ottawa, at the invitation of the Canadian Government and hosted by the International Development Research Centre. Prime Minister Trudeau received Mr Brandt and hosted a lunch for the Commissioners. Mr Ivan Head, President of IDRC, where the meeting was held, participated along with Mr Thorvald Stoltenberg as special guests. (Dr Lubbers, now the Dutch Prime Minister, intended to be at the meeting as a special guest, but had to change his plans at the last minute.) Commissioners also met with the Parliamentary Action Group on North–South Issues for a panel discussion in the House of Commons. In a concentrated three days' deliberations, the Commissioners adopted the final text of the Memorandum. (Commissioners not present at the meeting – Messrs Al-Hamad, Jamal, Palme, and Pisani – had submitted their suggestions in writing and are in agreement with the final text. As noted, Peter Peterson did not participate in the preparation of the Memorandum.)

The Chairman informed the public of the Memorandum at an Ottawa press conference on 15 December 1982, and a press statement was issued. UN Secretary General Javier Perez de Cuellar, it was announced, would receive the first copy of the new Memorandum.

Reactions

Public response to the Report was such that its members continued to meet and, after the disappointing outcome of the North–South Summit meeting at Cancun, Mexico, decided to make another appeal for urgent action to deal with the most critical issues and prepare the way for world recovery.

Public meetings in The Hague in May 1981 and in Berlin in 1982 attracted wide interest and 10,000 people came to a 'lobby on Brandt' on Parliament in London at about the same time. At the United Nations Special Session of the General Assembly, the statements of forty countries referred to the Report. The International Metal Workers Federation made the Report the main topic of their World Congress, as did the Junior Chambers of Commerce at their Berlin meeting. A vast number of articles, comments, reviews, studies and dissertations have been published or are being undertaken. (A draft bibliography and a detailed

166

index to the Report have been prepared by IBIDI and are available on request.)

The Report has been discussed by parliaments in several countries, task forces have been established, for example in Canada, and some other governments have revised their policy guidelines in light of the Report (Federal Republic of Germany, United Kingdom, Switzerland).

Seminars

In cooperation with and organised by the German Friedrich-Ebert Foundation—which also published *Towards one World?*, a collection of responses to the Report—seminars for high-level government officials were held in Bangkok, Bogota, Mexico City and Brazil. They were attended by invited Commissioners and key policy makers. A fifth seminar is still to be held in Zimbabwe.

Other Contacts

The Chairman and the Commissioners discussed the Report at numerous public meetings and with political leaders. Mr Brandt and Mr Jamal, for example, participated in a meeting of the European Association of Development Institutes in Budapest, which was attended by researchers from various parts of Europe, and thus gave them an opportunity to renew earlier contacts, especially with Eastern European experts. Olof Palme discussed the Report at various meetings in the Scandinavian countries and at a meeting of the International Communications Institute held in Ottawa in October 1980. Mr Heath and Mr Ramphal spoke at a large number of meetings too numerous to list in detail. All members of the Commission continue to receive more speaking initiatives than they can accept. The Report prompted many groups and organisations to increase their activities in the area of North–South relations. Even in the United States, where the initial impact had been very limited, there is now a growing grassroots movement centred on the Brandt Commission Research (Inc.) group, which provides public information on the work of the ICIDI and its international development objectives (BCR, PO Box 2619, North Canton, Ohio, 44720). Its initiators, James Bernard Quilligan and Jerry W. Baber, provided valuable technical support at the Ottawa meeting.

Acknowledgements

The Commissioners have received support and advice from many different groups and individuals. Ideas and encouragements have come from political leaders, national and international organisations, religious groups and trade unions, as well as other non-governmental organisations, research institutions—in particular the Centro de Estudios del Tercer Mundo, Mexico, and its President, Luis Echeverria—and universities. Many concerned citizens have contacted the Commissioners and IBIDI with valuable suggestions and proposals. Sincere appreciation and gratitude go to all of them.

The Commission owes a particular debt to the Commonwealth Secretariat in London, which provided a wealth of technical and logistic support.

The International Development Research Centre in Ottawa also provided invaluable help with its dedicated staff and by the facilities it made available during and after the Commission's final meeting.

Financial Contributions

The governments of Denmark, the Netherlands, Norway, Sweden, United Kingdom, and the OPEC Fund supported the follow-up work through untied contributions. The governments of Canada (local costs), Germany (FR), the Netherlands, Kuwait, and the Commission of the European Communities paid for travel to and local costs at the meetings. The German Marshall Fund of the United States will support some additional follow-up, such as the distribution of this Memorandum.

Possible Future Activities

A joint meeting of members of both the Brandt Commission and the Palme Commission may be held later in 1983. (Besides Mr Palme, Mr Mori and Mr Ramphal were also members of the Palme Commission.)

Notes

1 SDRs or Special Drawing Rights are international reserve assets created by the International Monetary Fund and allocated to members as a supplement to other reserves. All IMF members and some other designated holders may hold SDRs. They may use the SDR in a variety of transactions by agreement with each other. Members in balance of payments need may use SDRs to acquire foreign exchange; in such a case a member designated by the Fund provides currency in exchange for SDRs.

The valuation and interest rate of the SDR is based on the market exchange and interest rates of a basket of five currencies: the US dollar, the French franc, the Deutschmark, the pound sterling and the Japanese yen. Members pay interest to the Fund on the balance of their holding below their allocation, that is, when they use SDRs in transactions with others; and receive interest when their holding is above their allocation, that is, when they accept additional SDRs from others.

2 OECD, 1982(b).

3 Speech to the Annual Meeting of the IMF and World Bank, Toronto, September 1982.

4 World Bank, 1982(b).

5 Holsen *et al.*, 1976. See also UNCTAD 1982.

6 Morgan Guaranty Trust Company, 1982. OECD 1982(b) attributes ½ per cent of the downward revision of its 1983 OECD growth forecast to declining imports by non-OECD countries.

7 Bank for International Settlements, 1982.

8 Witteveen, 1982.

9 de Larosière, 1982.

10 The Report (p. 240) spoke of 'increasing concern that the international capital market and the private commercial banks, in the absence of intermediation by public institutions, can no longer be counted on to conduct the recycling process unassisted'. Without

'positive measures by governments and international institutions' the result would be 'a further decline of world economic activity and the threat of a serious crisis in the capital markets'. See also, e.g., World Bank, 1981(b).

11 Wallich, 1980.

12 Bank for International Settlements, *op. cit.*

13 World Bank estimates, cited by the President of the World Bank in his address to the GATT Ministerial Meeting, Geneva, November 1982.

14 IMF and private banking sources. An accurate estimate is impossible until some months after the year's end. There is a good deal of unpublicised as well as publicised lending. The one thing that seems certain is a sharp break in mid-1982 in the upward trend of lending which had prevailed earlier. OECD 1982(b) projects a $15 billion decline in net private capital flows to developing countries between 1981–83, of which $10 billion are declines in net bank lending.

15 Williamson, 1982

16 Cited *ibid.*

17 e.g. Killick (ed.), 1982.

18 e.g. Avramović, 1982; Khatkate (ed.), 1982; Killick, *op. cit.*; Williamson, *op. cit.*

19 Williamson, *op. cit.*

20 US Treasury, 1982.

21 World Bank, 1982(a).

22 World Bank, 1980.

23 World Bank. 1981(a).

24 OECD, 1982(a). The figures are for 1981. They fluctuate somewhat from year to year; thus Japan's was 0.32 in 1980.

25 World Bank, 1981(a).

26 World Bank, 1982(a).

27 See OECD, *op. cit.*

28 Witteveen, 1980.

29 e.g. Williamson, 1980.

30 e.g. Rohatyn, 1982.

31 World Bank, 1981(b).

32 IMF, 1982(b).

33 UNIDO, 1980.

34 World Bank, 1981(b).

35 Commonwealth Secretariat, 1982(b). Where not otherwise indicated, most data in this chapter are taken from this source and works there cited.

36 Wolf, 1982.

37 Data in this and the two previous paragraphs mainly from World Bank, 1982(b).
38 FAO, 1981.
39 Ibid.
40 UN World Food Council, 1982.
41 Deagle *et al.*, 1981; International Energy Agency, 1982.
42 e.g. World Bank, 1981(b).

References

The following are the principal sources of data and background material in the text.

D. Avramović, 'The Role of the IMF: The Disputes, the Qualifications and the Future', Paper presented to the North–South Roundtable, Tokyo/Oiso, 1982.

D. Badger and R. Belgrave, 'Oil Supply and Price: What Went Right in 1980?', *Energy Paper* No. 2, Policy Studies Institute and Royal Institute of International Affairs, London, 1982.

Bank for International Settlements, *Fifty-Second Annual Report*, Basle, June 1982.

Bank of England, *Quarterly Bulletin*, September 1982.

A. Carron, 'Financial Crises', Paper prepared for Brookings Panel on Economic Activity, Washington DC, September 1982.

Commission of the European Communities, 'Memorandum on the Community's Development Policy', COM (82) 640 Final, Brussels, October 1982.

Commonwealth Secretariat, *The North–South Dialogue: Making it Work*, Report of the Commonwealth Expert Group on the Negotiating Process, London, August 1982(a).

——, *Protectionism: Threat to International Order - The Impact on Developing Countries*, London, July 1982(b).

E. Deagle *et al.*, 'Energy in the 1980s: An Analysis of Recent Studies', *Occasional Papers* No. 4, Group of Thirty, New York, 1981.

FAO, *Agriculture Toward 2000*, Rome, 1981.

Group of Thirty, *Annual Report*, New York, 1982.

J. Holsen *et al.*, 'The Less Developed Countries and the International Monetary Mechanism', *American Economic Review*, May 1976.

Institut francais des relations internationales, *Les Pays Les Plus Pauvres. Quelle cooperation pour quel developpement?*, Paris, 1981.

——, *The State of the World Economy 1982*, Macmillan, London, 1982.

International Energy Agency, *World Energy Outlook*, OECD, Paris, 1982.

International Monetary Fund, 'External Indebtedness of Developing Countries', *Occasional Papers 3*, Washington DC, May 1981.

——, *Survey*, Washington DC, 5 April 1982(a).

——, *World Economic Outlook*, Washington DC, 1982(b).

D. Khatkhate (ed.), 'National and International Aspects of Financial Policies in LDCs', *World Development*, Special Issue, September 1982.

T. Killick (ed.), *Adjustment and Financing in the Developing World*, International Monetary Fund in Association with the Overseas Development Institute (London), Washington DC, 1982.

J. de Larosière, Address in Paris, April 1982, cited in IMF *Survey*, 5 April 1982, p. 99.

R. S. McNamara, Address to the Society for International Development, Baltimore, September 1982.

Morgan Guaranty Trust Company, *World Financial Markets*, New York, October, 1982.

OECD, *Development Cooperation* 1982 Review, Report of the Chairman of the Development Assistance Committee, Paris, November 1982(a).

——, *Economic Outlook* No. 32, Paris, December 1982(b).

F. Rohatyn, 'The State of the Banks', *New York Review of Books*, 4 November 1982.

J. Tumlir, 'International Economic Order: Can the Trend be Reversed?', *The World Economy*, Vol. 5, No. 1, March 1982.

UNCTAD, *Trade and Development Report 1982*, Geneva, 1982.

UNIDO, *Mineral Processing in Developing Countries*, Vienna, 1980.

UN World Food Council, 'World Food Security and Market Stability: A Developing Country-owned Reserve', WFC/1982/5, Rome, March 1982.

United States Treasury, *US Participation in the Multilateral Development Banks in the 1980s*, Washington DC, February 1982.

H. Wallich, 'LDC Debt – To Worry or Not to Worry?', Address to the 59th Annual Meeting of the Bankers' Association for Foreign Trade, Boca Raton, Florida, 2 June 1982.

J. Williamson, 'The Why and How of Funding LDC Debt', Pontificia Universidade Catolica de Rio de Janeiro, June 1980.

——, *The Lending Policies of the International Monetary Fund,* Institute for International Economics, Washington DC, August 1982.

H. J. Witteveen, 'Outlook for Investment Banking', Address to a *Financial Times* conference, Colombo, 4 September 1980.

——, 'Growing Financial Interdependence and Monetary Cooperation', Statement in New York, 7 October 1982.

M. Wolf, 'Worms in the Trade Apple', *Financial Times*, 26 October 1982.

World Bank, *World Development Report 1980*, Washington DC, 1980.

——, *Accelerated Development in Sub-Saharan Africa*, Washington DC, 1981(a).

——, *World Development Report 1981*, Washington DC, 1981(b).

——, *IDA in Retrospect*, Washington DC, 1982(a).

——, *World Development Report 1982*, Washington DC, 1982(b).